D0261049

Please return this book on or before the date shown above. To renew go to www.essex.gov.uk/libraries, ring 0845 603 7628 or go to any Essex library.

Essex County Council

HOW TO READ
INDUSTRIAL BRITAIN

HOW TO READ
INDUSTRIAL
BRITAIN

A GUIDE TO THE MACHINES,
SITES & ARTEFACTS THAT SHAPED BRITAIN

TIM COOPER

EBURY

10 9 8 7 6 5 4 3 2 1

Published in 2011 by Ebury Press, an imprint of Ebury Publishing

A Random House Group Company

The Random House Group Limited Reg. No. 954009

Address for companies within The Random House Group Limited can be found at
www.randomhouse.co.uk

A CIP catalogue record for this book is available from the British Library

The Random House Group Limited supports the Forest Stewardship Council®
(FSC®), the leading international forest certification organisation. All our titles that
are printed on Greenpeace approved FSC® certified paper carry the FSC® logo. Our
paper procurement policy can be found at www.randomhouse.co.uk/environment

ISBN 978 0 09 192998 5

Designed by David Fordham
Typeset by Palimpsest Book Production Ltd, Falkirk, Stirlingshire

Printed and bound in the UK by CPI Mackays, Chatham. ME5 8TD

To buy books by your favourite authors and register for offers visit
www.randomhouse.co.uk

Contents

For Pauline, with love

Acknowledgements

My thanks go to Sarah Kent, Steve and Kate Sly and Richard Taylor for bringing me and this book together. That was some party.

Photo Acknowledgements

Plate section: p 1 top © Ann Pickford / Alamy; bottom © Louis Atherton / Alamy; p 2 top © Stunning images / Alamy, bottom © Robert Brook / photolibrary; p 3 top © Steve Frost / Alamy, bottom © mambo / Alamy; p 4 top © Alan Novelli / Alamy; bottom © Jane Tregelles / Alamy; p 5 top © Neil Setchfield / Alamy, bottom © Alistair Laming / Alamy; p 6 top © John Peter Photography / Alamy, bottom © Stan Pritchard / Alamy; p 7 top © Britain on View / photolibrary, bottom © Mike Robinson / Alamy; p 8 top © Tony West / photolibrary, bottom © Cooter / Alamy

Illustration p 7, 37, 67, 97, 133 © Petrafler

INTRODUCTION: READING THE INDUSTRIAL PAST

WHY NOW?

From the perspective of the early 21st century, Industrial Britain increasingly seems part of our past experience rather than our present. In other words, rather than being a living part of the world we know, it has become part of our common heritage. In the single generation between its Prime Ministers Margaret Thatcher and Tony Blair, Britain was transformed from an economy based on manufacture to one that is dependent on the provision of services. The consequence was industrial decline followed by urban regeneration aimed at creating a new, post-industrial society. Meanwhile the century in which the developments of the Industrial Revolution reached their peak – the 20th – is itself now history.

Quite apart from the disappearance of many of Britain's traditional industries, and their associated physical remains, the evidence of our having become a post-industrial society is in the very language we use. It is now common, for instance, to speak of 'the tourist industry' or 'the credit card industry'; a bank loan is described as a 'product', and question and answer sessions take place in a 'workshop'. To previous generations, who grew up in a world where money was generated by making things, such talk would have made little sense. Something has clearly changed.

Yet the profound changes that have occurred in British society over the past generation have taken place against a physical backdrop that was created by the Industrial Revolution. In short, industrialisation created the material world in which we live. It moulded the landscape of modern Britain and left a powerful legacy not just in the remaining monuments of industry itself but in our houses, roads, railway stations, parks and pubs. The first generation of industrial archaeologists recognised the paradox that, although much is familiar, in terms of collective memory the world of the Industrial Revolution is becoming to us as distant as that of ancient Rome.

Most of us have little direct contact with, or experience of, the industrial foundations on which our own society has been built. So if you have ever looked out of the window of a car or train and wondered what that strange conical brick structure is; or wandered around your converted urban apartment and wondered what the building was once used for; or passed an old factory building on the way to work and got the feeling that it is something at once familiar but becoming increasingly unknown – then this book is for you.

What Do We Mean by Industrial Britain?

An industrial society can be briefly summarised as one which developed the ability to move away from economic dependence on agriculture, developed large-scale exploitation of energy reserves and manufacturing in metal, and significantly increased the scale of production and accumulation of capital, allowing greater levels of investment.

The social and economic changes that came with industrialisation were profound and can be compared with the impact brought by the introduction of farming in prehistory and the formation of city-states in the ancient world. From the viewpoint of the 21st century we are justified in using Industrial Britain as an all-embracing historical description in the same way that we would use, for example, Bronze Age Britain.

The development of the first industrial society occurred in Britain in the mid 18th century, as evidenced first by the mechanisation of the textiles industries. Next came the adoption of coal as a universal source of energy that enabled, first, expansion of metalworking and, second, the production of steam power, which in turn allowed a huge leap forward to take place in the scale of manufacture. The physical setting for mechanisation and change in scale of production was the factory system. Together, these changes have traditionally been termed the Industrial Revolution.

Starting around 1850 a further set of changes occurred, sometimes referred to as 'the second industrial revolution'. These included the application of steam power to locomotion and, eventually, the generation of electricity. In addition there was the further development of the factory system into methods of mass production, the ultimate products of which were domestic appliances and the motor car. Another way of looking at these phases is that the first was concerned with changes in what are termed primary forms of manufacture. These included the mining of coal, the manufacture of textiles and metals and the making of machines. The second saw the large-scale manufacture of everyday items such as household goods.

One of the most significant by-products of industrialisation was the population explosion that occurred during the 19th and 20th centuries and which involved a great movement of people from rural areas to crowded accommodation in town and cities. In turn this led to the creation of a new gradation within society – traditionally termed the 'working class' – which exercised as powerful an influence on the development of British culture as had the rise of the merchant class in the previous era.

Whether or not we agree with the use of the word 'revolution', the changes that occurred during the process of industrialisation were profound and left a substantial and varied legacy of material remains. These include individual monuments such as the Iron Bridge in Shropshire and whole areas like the Derwent Valley in Derbyshire, birthplace of the mechanised textiles industry. It would not be unfair to say, however, that the richness of this heritage, and its importance in world history, have until recently gained greater recognition outside the British Isles than within.

Reading Industrial Britain

⌗ The premise of this book, therefore, is that although the industrial world is fast receding into the past, it provided the foundations on which modern Britain is built and its evidence is all around us. Its main aim is as an aid to understanding how individual sites, buildings and monuments formed part of the wider landscape of Industrial Britain. It is based on the belief that only when taken in context can the significance of individual features be properly appreciated. In many cases this is far from obvious. It is a paradox, for example, that while we might start looking for evidence of the industrial past in towns and cities, some of the heartlands of industrial activity are to be found in what are now rural settings such as the Derbyshire Peak District and the Cornish peninsula.

Another pervasive theme in the discovery of Industrial Britain is how much in the physical environment was designed to look like something else, something from a different age or with a different use. It is always worth asking why this might have been done and how readily historians of the future will be able to distinguish between, say, a Jacobean manor house and a Victorian railway station. The deception was often quite intentional. Artifice, after all, was one of the foundations on which Industrial Britain was built. As such, the book can be seen as a sort of 'guide to industrial tourism' which, as well as uncovering the significance of monumental structures and landscape features, will help to uncover layers of meaning in the everyday and the seemingly familiar. A book like this cannot hope to be a comprehensive gazetteer of Industrial Britain. Rather, its primary purpose is to encourage a closer look at a disappearing world around us, a second glance out of the car window at the crumbling factory next to the railway bridge, or the pub at the end of a terraced row of houses. It is hoped that the examples of evidence from Industrial Britain that are highlighted in the book will form a starting point for readers' own discoveries in the world around them.

The structure of the book takes its form from the belief that the defining characteristics of Industrial Britain were the way in which our predecessors harnessed new forms of energy to develop innovative materials, on a previously unimagined scale, from which they mass-produced goods in conditions of highly organised labour. In turn, this revolution in the way things were made stimulated a parallel revolution in transport, together with new ways of living together. While the 'industrial' part of the book's title has to do with the rise of factories and developments in technology, 'Britain' is concerned with the types of community, landscape and culture that industrialism was fundamental in creating.

In terms of chronology – which is always fairly arbitrary – Industrial Britain is seen as encompassing a period from roughly 1750, by which time coal reserves were starting to be employed in the mass production of iron, to 1990, when the pit closure programme, coming on top of the decline in manufacturing during the previous decade, brought about the effective end of this phase in our history. In reality, no historical process can be so readily confined, so developments from outside of this date range will occasionally be examined where they are relevant to the overall picture.

Many of the traditional works of industrial archaeology have focused on icons of the Industrial Revolution such as the Iron Bridge or New Lanark Mills. While these will certainly not be neglected in the discussion that follows, particular emphasis will be given to buildings and features that, through conversion and change of function, are passing into post-industrial use and which therefore encapsulate the profound economic and social changes that are taking place in the current generation. These changes are perhaps most evident in the conversion of former factories and warehouses in the old industrial cities to new uses ranging from apartments and retail outlets to pubs and night-clubs. Even as its meaning slowly fades into the past, the legacy of Industrial Britain is all around us.

CHAPTER ONE

POWER

Harnessing readily available sources of power on a large scale was fundamental to the process of industrialisation. In the early stages it was one of the main traditional sources – water – that was exploited most fully. Meanwhile, the fuel for the heat that was required to perform industrial processes, such as the production of metals, was initially provided by charcoal from the forests in which Britain once abounded. However, even by the 16th century timber supplies were becoming scarce and government was turning its attention to conserving resources for naval shipbuilding. By the beginning of the 18th century this had led to a shift towards coal, which until this time had been used only on a limited scale. Purification of coal in the form of coke led to its wider application to manufacturing industry.

Then, in an almost alchemical coming together of energy in the form of coal and water to produce steam power, the Industrial Revolution was born. Steam power went on to have almost countless applications, not least in originally providing the means of generating electricity, which itself became the indispensable source of power behind the technological leap sometimes known as the 'second industrial revolution' of the late 19th and early 20th centuries. At the same time, coal found its life prolonged as a fuel source well into the 20th century through its derivatives in the form of gas and oil.

WATER

For over 300 years, small-scale industrial processes in Britain were powered by water. Indeed, water had been used for milling and powering bellows in iron smelting since the Middle Ages. As Britain moved towards full-scale industrial development, water continued to be harnessed as the main source of power, and significant developments in the technology of power transfer occurred in the mid 17th century. In the late 18th century increasing efforts were made to improve the efficiency of water wheels, which became vital to the early development of the factory system of production (see below).

It is no surprise, therefore, that some of the first centres of large-scale industrial production were in the area of the lower Pennines, where fast-flowing streams could be harnessed to provide power to manufacturing processes. The most dramatic example was Sheffield, which during the 18th century developed from a regional market centre into one of Britain's first industrial towns. Its geographical position at the foot of a number of hills from which descended racing watercourses meant that its narrow valleys were home to no fewer than 150 water-powered workshops by the end of the century.

Water Wheels and the Tilt Hammer

▣ As early as the end of the 15th century, water wheels were no longer confined to uses such as milling corn, but were being used to operate bellows at iron foundries. Over time, the application of water-generated power to

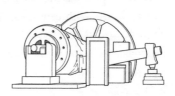

The Tilt Hammer

ironworking led to the invention of the tilt hammer, which meant that large quantities of wrought iron could be worked quickly and efficiently. In turn, this was to lead to the technological developments that allowed the mass production of steel, the quintessential product of the Industrial Revolution (see p. 44).

The development of water power in the area of ironworking, and the invention of the tilt hammer, had a particular impact in Sheffield and its surrounding district, where numerous workshops produced agricultural tools and the raw materials of the cutlery industry. There were a number of ways in which tilt hammers took the power generated by water wheels and transferred it to the working of metal, but each method consisted essentially of an iron head and wooden haft coming down on an iron anvil and delivering light blows in rapid succession. Though some water-powered forges and their associated tilt hammers survive, in many parts of England, in particular, the remaining evidence is in the form of the 'hammer ponds', which were used to manage the power of watercourses to enable continuous efficient operation.

As the scale of metalworking increased, water supply was also crucial for the working of blast furnaces (see p. 50), whose processes required long periods of continuous work. By the time industrialisation was in full swing in the mid 19th century, water power was being used for a range of industrial tasks. For example, at Coniston in the English Lake District evidence survives in the landscape of no fewer than 13 water wheels employed there for the processing of the copper quarried from the hills in the 1850s (see p. 55).

Water Mills

⊡ There was little technological development in water wheels until the mid 18th century, when experiments proved that the overshot wheel was significantly more efficient than the undershot (see diagrams). The greatest development in water power systems occurred in the textile mills and factories that were among the greatest users of power in the industrial period. Indeed, the importance of water-generated power to the

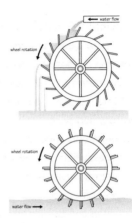

Overshot and Undershot Waterwheel

development of the factory system is reflected in the common name for such buildings – *mills*. The earliest factories conveyed power from the water wheels by way of wooden drums, which used a leather belt to drive the machinery directly. Over time this basic system developed into one where the water wheels drove a variety of different machinery using a combination of horizontal and vertical line shafts connected by toothed gears.

Turbines

⊡ Otherwise, the application of water power to factory machinery remained relatively static until the early 20th century, when water wheels were gradually replaced with turbines driving vertical shafts, such as those installed at Quarry Bank in 1905. In most situations, turbines proved themselves more efficient than the traditional water wheel.

COAL

Until the middle of the18th century, charcoal made from burnt wood had been the main fuel employed by industry. However, deforestation coupled with government legislation aimed at conserving valuable timber supplies for use in shipbuilding led to increasing use of coal, which, by the end of the century, had become Britain's most important natural resource. Unremarkable though it may be in appearance, coal has rightly been described as one of the 'mainsprings' of the Industrial Revolution, providing energy for the fashioning of metals and the generation of steam (see p. 19). Since naturally occurring impurities can cause problems when it is burnt, it was in its purified state, as coke, that coal was first used on an industrial scale.

The most dramatic increase in use came in the 1850s, when engineering improvements meant that it could replace coke as the main fuel for railway locomotives. By the turn of the century, 200 million tonnes of coal were being mined each year, the vast majority of it fuelling the steam engines that gave power to factories, and the locomotives that provided the backbone of the transport system (see p. 110). From the first quarter of the 20th century onwards, the final major phase of industrialisation was made possible by the burning of coal, first for the production of gas and then the generation of electricity. Peak production, of 287 million tonnes, was reached in 1913, a time when the number of men employed in the industry also peaked at over 1.13 million, or about 9 per cent of Britain's total male labour force.

Already, by the end of the First World War, output was in

decline. Over 2,500 collieries were still in operation in 1924, but at the outbreak of the Second World War this had reduced to 1,870. An industry hit hard by overcapacity in the first three-quarters of the 20th century was dealt the fatal blow by a combination of cheap imports and government policy in the decade up to 1990.

Geographical Distribution

🔳 Despite the growing significance of coal production, throughout its entire history it was an industry of small units. In 1913 there were 1,439 colliery companies in Britain, owning on average no more than two pits each. Some mines were operated by combined concerns, for example companies that also operated blast furnaces or engineering works. At the same time many operators were small-scale, supplying local markets and providing fuel for individual factories.

One of the first large-scale areas of production had been that part of the Midlands to the immediate west of Birmingham situated on the great seam of so-called 'Staffordshire thick coal'. When this was burnt in quantity, the effect, combined with the numerous metal workings of the area, led to its enduring infamous description as the 'Black Country'.

A notable feature of the first quarter of the 20th century was the interest taken in exploitation of coal resources by the old landed estates, a phenomenon that greatly influenced the industrial and social development of large areas of northern and midland England in particular. The other area that developed dramatically in response to increasing coal production was the valleys of South Wales. One of the most prominent centres was Rhondda, where coal-mining had commenced on an industrial scale in the 1850s. By the end of the 19th century it had become one of the biggest coal-producing areas in the world, with over

50 working collieries crammed into a valley 16 miles (26km) long. By the time of the depression of the 1920s a rural population that had stood at about 950 in 1851 had burgeoned to an incredible 169,000. At its high point, one out of every 10 people in Wales was employed in the coal industry and a great many more were dependent upon it less directly.

Extraction Techniques

BELL PITS

The earliest, small-scale coal-mining operations were in the form of 'bell pits'. By this method seams close to the surface were worked successively, the miners moving from one part of the seam into the next at the stage where the roof was in danger of collapsing. The circular remains of such workings are particularly visible in parts of Yorkshire and Shropshire.

DRIFT MINES

A development in surface mining techniques was the drift mine, by which seams were exploited by means of an incline, or drift, driven into their slope. The impediment to more economic mining of coal was the danger inherent in working at greater depth and the problems involved in mine drainage and ventilation, not to mention the increased costs. The greatest technological advance, therefore, was the introduction of steam-driven pump engines into the mining industry (see p. 19).

PIT PROPS

For much of the industry's history, the actual technique of mining changed remarkably little. Miners, or 'colliers', would lie on their side and use a small pick to cut into the lower face of the coal seam as far as they could reach. The next stage was to bore holes into the top of the seam using hand drills, all the while pulling a small cart behind into which the coal was deposited. Where conditions allowed, explosives were used in combination with drills. In order to prevent the roof of the mine collapsing, miners would insert timber props as they progressed along the seam. For much of the 19th century, men were paid according to the number of full carts, or tubs, they produced which were duly weighed at the surface. It was common practice for the collier to employ other workers to haul his tub and insert his pit props – until the introduction of legislation in 1842, these workers were often his wife and children.

As demand for coal increased, pits were sunk ever deeper, a development which was greatly facilitated by improved methods of drainage and ventilation (see p. 15). The last generation of coal-mines, sunk around the turn of the 20th century, were often extremely deep in order to exploit the vast sub-surface resources that remained. In these circumstances miners could find themselves descending as much as 3,000 feet (900m) before travelling to work at a coal-face that could be over a mile (1.6km) away.

MAN RIDERS

Men travelled to the working face, and between the seams of a single mine, in so-called 'man riders', small rail-mounted cars operated initially by compressed air and sometimes later by diesel locomotives.

MECHANICAL EXTRACTION

Mechanisation of the coal industry began in earnest in the late 19th century. Since the use of steam engines was out of the question below ground, machinery was driven originally by compressed air and later, increasingly, by electricity. The danger of sparks causing the explosion of flammable gases meant that electric machinery was not widely introduced until 1904, when safer alternating current appliances became available. The most widely used coal-cutting machines employed a toothed disc, a method which did not substantially change until the later 20th century, by which time huge machines travelled along the coal-face ripping into the seams and removing the coal.

Drainage, Ventilation and Safety

DRAINAGE TUNNELS

When the demand for coal began to rise in the early 18th century the depth to which mines could be sunk was restricted by the difficulty of keeping them free of water. The earliest attempts consisted of drainage tunnels, known in various parts of the country as 'water gates', 'adits' or 'soughs'. However, these could only ever be of use in operations of limited depth. It was the application of steam technology (see below) that allowed mines to go deeper in the search for coal and that, coincidentally, set the ball rolling for the entire transformation of Britain from an agricultural society to the 'first industrial nation'.

SHAFT VENTILATION

Whereas flooding and drainage were problems common to all mining operations, the digging of coal presented particular dangers in the form of gases that were released, the most danger-ous of which was the explosive mixture of methane and air encountered in deep mines and known as 'firedamp'. The chal-lenge to mining engineers was to ensure adequate air circulation around the mine. This was usually achieved by a combination of fans, which drew stale air out of the mine, and chimneys allowing fresh air to be drawn in. All coal-mines therefore had at least two shafts, which were used both for ventilation and for access. The so-called 'up cast shaft', through which the fans drew air out of the workings, was also used for the lift apparatus that provided the mine's main entrance and exit. Similarly, the 'down cast shaft' usually had metal rungs attached to the inside to allow escape in case of emergency.

SAFETY LAMPS
Regardless of these improvements, for its entire history coal-mining remained a dangerous activity. Between 1835 and 1850 there were 643 coal-mine explosions in the North East of England alone, and this was despite the introduction of the so-called 'safety lamp' invented by Humphrey Davy in 1815. Records for South Wales show that, on average, between 1868 and 1919 the death of a miner occurred every six hours and an injury every two minutes. Sparks from early signalling and electrical equipment were to blame for several violent explosions; even an isolated spark could ignite a pocket of firedamp, which could start off a coal-dust explosion. Before entering the 'cage' by which they descended the mine shaft, men would be searched by the 'banksman', so-called because he 'banked' any items such as cigarettes, matches or foil wrappings which could cause sparks and hence an explosion. After entering the cage the miner would hand the banksman a 'tally', or token, which in case of emergency would show how many men were left underground.

The Pithead

The few surviving surface remains of Britain's coal industry are mainly in the form of the pithead gear that was the focus of any working mine. In the earliest operations, removal of buckets, tubs and carts full of coal was achieved by the so-called 'horse gin', the word gin being a contraction of 'engine', the common term in use at the time for a machine. These consisted of a circular winding mechanism, similar to a windlass, which was turned by a horse driven round a circular track.

As mines became deeper, vertical shafts became the normal

form of access, and these were obviously unsuited to this form of mechanism. The system that developed in its place was the familiar one whereby cages were lowered and raised by a winding mechanism mounted above the shaft on a headstock. Such mechanisms became one of the main applications of steam engines at mines, the others being the drainage and ventilation systems. The earliest headstocks were wooden-framed, but these were generally replaced by constructions made of rolled-steel girders. From the mid 20th century, winding gear was increasingly powered by electricity.

It was not until the 1930s that pithead baths were generally introduced for the use of the miners at the end of shifts. Many such buildings were commissioned by the Miners Welfare Fund and were built in the modernist architectural style popular at the time. Other pithead buildings might include a canteen and medical centre, these too usually being provided by the welfare fund.

Pithead

Transport Systems

HORSE-DRAWN TRAMS
Since coal was a bulk commodity, which needed to be transported in large quantities, the development of the coal industry and of transport systems went hand in hand. At the local level this was usually in the form of the horse-drawn tramways, originally with wooden tracks, which were common in the mining areas of the North East of England. Such tracked transport systems provided lower friction for heavy loads and thus meant that coal could be moved more efficiently and speedily over distance. Some tramways

covered large distances in order to transport coal to special ports – called 'staithes' – at which the coal was transferred from wagon to vessels for shipment, in particular to the rapidly growing market that was London.

IRON RAILWAYS

It was at Coalbrookdale in Shropshire (see p. 38–9) that iron rails were first manufactured and used. In combination with iron wheels, these allowed even more efficient transport of coal and, in time, the linking of coal-mining operations to canal and railway transport systems (see p. 88). Indeed, one of the main spurs to the development of the canal system was the need for efficient exploitation of coal resources.

Coal Mining Landscapes

◫ Although the coal-mines left relatively few visible remains, the industry had a much wider impact on the landscape of Britain than just the pits themselves. Transport systems frequently developed around the collieries, as did – with even greater lasting significance – entire communities (see p. 139). In South Wales and Scotland in particular this meant the rapid expansion of former rural populations. In many areas of midland and northern England it led to the creation of entirely new communities, often on land owned by the aristocracy who, from the early 20th century, sought to cash in on coal to counteract declining income from land. Whilst in all of these areas there has been significant dereliction, particularly since the 1990s, the settlement patterns that the coal industry produced can still be readily discerned, be it in the strung-out rows of houses of the Welsh valleys or the 'garden villages' of Derbyshire, Yorkshire and Northumberland (see p. 142).

STEAM

Water and coal may sound mundane today, but the fusion of water power with the energy of coal in order to harness the power of steam was arguably the most revolutionary development of the entire industrial period. Within a relatively short time the power of steam was brought to bear on almost every aspect of industrialisation. The first generation of commercial steam engines helped solve the problem of draining deeper mines; the second powered the machines of the textile factories that almost single-handedly took Britain to the top of the world's economies.

More revolutionary still was the application of steam technology to locomotive power, and by the second half of the 19th century railways had become virtually synonymous with industrialisation. Finally, the second great technological leap of the industrial period – often referred to as the 'second industrial revolution' – was made possible by the burning of vast amounts of coal to produce steam that in turn drove the turbines used to generate electric power. Virtually every part of the material world we have inherited had its origin, therefore, in the successful exploitation of the scientific properties of steam.

Developments in Steam Engineering

Steam engines were developed initially as the solution to the problem of mine drainage, and half a century elapsed before they were put to work on anything else. This was partly due to the fact that, although the principles behind the expansive properties of steam were understood by the late 17th century, the level of engineering required to make productive engines lagged some way behind. In this respect the significance of the engineering genius of Thomas Newcomen is impossible to overestimate, and some regard his technological innovations as the most important single factor in propelling mankind into the modern, mechanised world. In turn, James Watt's improvements on Newcomen's designs enabled the successful application of rotary power, and the widespread employment of the engines developed by Watt and his collaborator Matthew Boulton is testimony to the abilities of Newcomen's successors. Indeed, the documentary evidence of sales of Boulton & Watt engines has been used as an indicator of the industrial impact of steam within industry in the late 18th century, as well as the emerging industrial geography of Britain.

Steam-generated rotary power brought about industry's most significant technological change, as the improved steam engines freed manufacturing processes not only from the unreliability of power supplies based on water alone, but even from the need for the emerging factories to be situated next to watercourses at all. This single aspect of the development of the steam engine meant that a whole new centre of the textile industry could be developed in the lowland plain of Lancashire, more convenient for both supplies of labour and access to markets, and virtually at a stroke a major component of the enduring industrial geography of Britain was put in place.

THE NEWCOMEN ENGINE

Thomas Newcomen (1663–1729) was an ironmonger from Dartmouth, in Devon, who set his mind to the problem of draining the Cornish tin mines and as a result came up with the world's first automatic steam engine in 1712. The engine worked by means of a piston – itself operated by the expansion of steam from

Newcomen Engine

nwater heated in a boiler – moving a balanced beam attached to the pump, which would carry out the drainage. The steam was then condensed by a stream of water within the cylinder, enabling the piston to be forced into its cylinder by atmospheric pressure. It was in reference to this process that Newcomen's machines were often called 'atmospheric engines'. By the early 1730s over 100 engines had been installed in Britain, the great majority employed in mine drainage.

THE BOULTON & WATT ENGINE

The Scottish engineer James Watt (1736–1819) discovered certain inefficiencies of the Newcomen engine while working on a model in his laboratory in Glasgow; he overcame them by developing a separate condenser, an innovation that was perhaps the greatest single improvement ever made to the steam engine. In 1773 Watt entered into partnership with the Birmingham toy manufacturer Matthew Boulton (1728–1809), constructing engines that consumed one third of the amount of coal used by the Newcomen machines. As such they met with immediate success in the tin mines of Cornwall, where coal was locally unavailable and therefore expensive.

Three further important improvements were made to steam engine design by James Watt in 1782. The first of these was to apply steam to both the top and bottom faces of the pistons, which meant that twice the power could be produced by the same cylinder volume. The second was better use of the expansive properties of steam, which resulted in further fuel savings by achieving the same amount of work with less steam. However, it was Watt's third improvement that represented the greatest technological leap forward: the provision of rotary power allowed all sorts of manufacturing machinery to be worked directly.

THE CORNISH BEAM ENGINE

One of the most widely adopted engine designs was that developed by Richard Trevithick (1771–1833), based on a prototype tested at Gwithian, in Cornwall, in 1812. Popular in the Cornish tin mines, and later with water supply and sewage companies, the Cornish beam engines were powerful, reliable and, since they operated at a significantly higher pressure, even more efficient than their predecessors. The numerous remaining stone-built engine houses constructed for these machines are the most distinctive features of the industrial landscape of the Cornish peninsula.

GEOGRAPHICAL DISTRIBUTION OF STEAM ENGINES

Detailed records survive enabling us to build up a picture of the distribution, both geographically and by industry, of the steam engines manufactured by the company of Boulton & Watt. These illustrate that much of the industrial geography of Britain as we know it today was already established by the end of the 18th century. Perhaps only Shropshire and Cornwall, which witnessed the decline in their iron and tin industries respectively, are over-represented. Otherwise, the engines were installed most widely at the textile mills of Lancashire, an area that continued to dominate the industrial landscape of Britain until the end of the 20th century.

Demand for the more efficient Boulton & Watt engines had been greatest in Cornwall, where geological factors meant that coal was expensive. However, within a century of the development of the rotary steam engine in 1782, there were almost 500 engines employed in the metal industries of Sheffield alone. In terms of national distribution by industry, over one third were employed in textile manufacture, with cotton-spinning factories accounting for almost 100 engines in 1800. Other significant users of steam power were the coal-mines that relied on them for drainage.

Further Technological Improvements

As early as the 1720s iron manufacturers in Coalbrookdale (see below) had started casting cylinders for Newcomen engines in iron instead of the traditional brass, which enabled use at higher pressure. However, the greatest improvement to boilers did not take place until Trevithick developed his 'Cornish' boiler in 1812. This remained the most popular design until the development in the 1840s of the 'Lancashire' boiler, consisting of a cylindrical unit with two flues, which provided a substantially increased heating surface and therefore greater power and efficiency. By the end of the 19th century the huge Lancashire textile mills were demanding increasingly higher power to drive their vast ranks of machinery and it was to the task of producing this that the improved technology was applied.

ELECTRICITY

The large-scale generation of electricity, the principles of which had been discovered by Thomas Faraday in 1831, enabled the final phase of industrialisation to take place. Together with the industrial application of gas that followed, it was the final and most significant use of coal to power the transformation of society. We now take electricity so much for granted that we can easily forget the extent to which it permeates modern life. For most of the 20th century it provided the main source of energy to the industries that in turn developed the standard of living on which we have come to depend. Electric power liberated industry from the constraints of the past, in particular from location near streams and coalfields, which characterised the earliest developments.

Until the very end of the 20th century, almost all of the electricity generated in Britain came from coal-fuelled power stations, maintaining the link between coal and industrial production which had been established in the 18th century. The large-scale industrial application of electricity commenced with the introduction of electrical dynamos at textile mills in the 1880s. Between the two world wars a combination of private and municipal enterprise, with increasing direction from central government, provided Britain with an infrastructure of power that put it at the forefront of industrial nations. In terms of manufacturing processes, electricity made it possible for each individual machine in a workshop or factory to have its own appropriate power supply, rather than being driven by a common – and often unwieldy – system of belt and line shafting that had been the norm hitherto. This in turn led to a degree of special-isation in mechanical and manufacturing processes that would have been hard to envisage in the heyday of Victorian engineer-ing. Ultimately, the harnessing of electricity to the needs of artificial light and domestic appliances led to the 21st-century world of mobile telecommunications and personal computing.

Individual Generating Plants

⚙ The first electricity generators were entirely private concerns, such as that installed by the armaments baron Sir William Armstrong at his home of Cragside in Northumberland in 1878. In the final two decades of the 19th century a number of privately owned generating stations came into operation, but most were small-scale and located close to their customers. Many provided power to particular industrial concerns, such as the one serving the coal-mine at Philadelphia, Co. Durham, established in 1906. Individual plants mainly used reciprocating steam engines, although one of the first to provide electricity for street lighting, the generator at Godalming in Surrey built in 1881, was powered by a traditional water wheel.

In the 1890s small-scale generating plants were built in a number of cities throughout the country, mainly to provide power for electric lighting or tram systems. However, large-scale developments were limited by the inability of the reciprocating steam engines – which turned the generators by either a belt drive or a direct-coupled crankshaft – to develop sufficient speed for efficient and stable electrical generation. The first textile mills to be powered electrically generated power on site, usually by means of steam turbines located in a separate power house. A notable feature of many of the early private generating stations was their distinctive architectural styles and detailing, incorporated to reflect the importance of the new source of power.

Municipal Generating Plants

⊠ The first municipal electricity plants were established in the 1880s and used steam engines, steam turbines or occasionally gas engines to drive generators supplying power for street lighting, tramways and industrial concerns. A notable landmark was the foundation of the London Electricity Supply Corporation in 1887, which generated electricity from what was arguably the country's first 'power station' at Deptford. Unlike most of the relatively small and modestly designed plants that were built around the same time, Deptford was the first of what might be called 'flagship' power stations. However, though its scale was impressive, when completed in 1891 it turned out to be something of a technological dead end. With generators based on the principles of S.Z. de Ferranti (1864–1930) it needed significant modification before it was able to generate a stable power supply to businesses and consumers in the area. In the long term, however, this early enterprise was a success and the building remained until 1992 when it was demolished to make way for the Millennium Quay housing development.

Power Stations

'Energy . . . is to be considered as a commodity which can be manu-
factured in a convenient form, distributed and sold.' (W.C. Unwin,
1893)

STEAM TURBINES

The problem encountered with the earliest reciprocating steam
engines that were used for generating electricity – insufficient
speed for efficient generation – was overcome in the mid 1880s
by the introduction of steam turbines. These were essentially the
same as those used in modern power stations, the turbines being
coupled directly to an alternator. The introduction of this new
technology led to the construction of a number of power stations
around the turn of the 20th century, most located near to the
railways, canals or harbours that could ensure a constant supply
of their primary fuel – coal. Some stations, such as Rugeley in
Staffordshire, were situated right next to the coal-mines which
supplied their fuel.

SUPER STATIONS

The 1919 Electricity (Supply) Act led to the building of the first
generation of so-called 'super stations' which included Stourport
(1927), Hams Hall 'A' (1929), Clarence Dock, Liverpool (1931)
and Ironbridge 'A' (1932). One of the latest to be built in this
round of construction, Battersea (1933), went on to achieve
enduring fame. For years the largest such installation in Europe,
its dramatic exterior – in many ways the direct descendant of the
flagship mills and factories of the previous century (p. 75) – was
designed by Sir Giles Gilbert Scott (1880–1960), heir to the
great Victorian family of architects, already celebrated for his
iconic red telephone box design and his work at Liverpool
Cathedral. Indeed, it would not be too much of an exaggeration

to view the great power stations of the inter-war period as the cathedrals of their age.

THE CENTRAL ELECTRICITY GENERATING BOARD

The second wave of construction commenced following the nationalisation of utilities in 1948 and the creation of the Central Electricity Generating Board. Despite inheriting over 300 generating plants the board invested heavily in ever larger stations, the sheer size of which made it an economic necessity for them to be located close to their source of fuel. It was for this reason that the Trent valley became the enduring 'power axis' of Britain below the Scottish border, being near to the huge coal reserves of the East Midlands and a constant supply of water for operational and cooling purposes. These huge construction projects included Drakelow, Willington and Staythorpe, with Castle Donington, opening in 1956, representing something of a landmark as the first power station to have 100 megawatt generating units. The design and architecture of these great plants said much for the optimism of post-war Britain in terms of its industrial strength and ability to plan for the needs of its people, and seemed to express the country's confident march towards modernity.

Improvements in technology meant that by the final quarter of the 20th century fewer than 100 stations nationally were supplying four times the amount of power that had been available at the time of nationalisation. Moves towards greater efficiency had actually commenced as early as 1952 with the construction of the oil-fired station Bankside 'B' by the Thames in London in 1952. Constructed to another flagship design by Sir Giles Gilbert Scott, this continued to supply power to large parts of the capital until its decommissioning in 1981 and conversion to the Tate Modern art gallery in time for the new millennium, opening in January 2000.

HYPERBOLIC COOLING TOWERS

The most distinctive feature of modern power stations is undoubtedly the hyperbolic cooling towers, by means of which water used for cooling the condensers is returned to its source at an appropriate temperature. The first of these were constructed at Lister Drive power station in Liverpool in the mid 1920s but were tiny in comparison with their soaring successors which are such a dominant component of the modern landscape of the Trent Valley.

The National Grid

▣ As the number of consumers of electricity increased, the current flowing in the mains system became heavier and the mains themselves longer. As a result the loss of power through voltage drop soon became a serious problem. The solution, first proposed by S.Z. de Ferranti, was to transmit an alternating current at high voltage which could later be reduced at local sub-stations and transformers in accordance with consumer needs. This development formed the basis of the electricity supply network operating at 400,000 and 275,000 volts known as the 'National Grid'.

Originally there was little standardisation in the industry, and companies provided alternating current (AC) or direct current (DC) at a range of voltages. The Electricity (Supply) Act of 1926 placed the industry under the overall supervision of the Central Electricity Board, which purchased

Pylon

electricity from generating companies and then distributed it by means of a national network through a system of local distributors. The result was a 4,000-mile (6,400km) network of power lines supported by huge steel 'pylons' that by 1933 was distributing power from over 100 of the larger generating stations. The creation of the National Grid, by which all power stations were connected, was a further impetus to their location in areas close to the source of fuel and the subsequent transmission of electricity over long distances by means of overhead power lines.

Uses of Electricity

In 1881, the same year that electricity was first used for public lighting in Britain, at Godalming in Surrey (see p. 24), incandescent electric lamps were installed in the House of Commons and rapidly became popular generally. While the earliest electricity concerns – such as the Edison company, which opened its Holborn Viaduct generating station in 1882 – supplied power mainly for street lighting, they soon started to offer supplies to private consumers. By the mid 1880s the monopoly of gas for street lighting was challenged for the first time by the commercial availability of electric arc and incandescent filament lamps. As a consequence throughout the 1890s small power stations were built in the larger towns in many parts of the country by electric light companies.

GAS

It was William Murdock (1754–1839), principal engineer in Cornwall for the company of Boulton & Watt, who first demonstrated the combustible properties of a mixture of coal gas and air. In 1792 he successfully lit a room in his house in

Redruth using coal gas burners, and in the following year Boulton & Watt's Soho Foundry in Birmingham was entirely lit by Murdock's wonderful new invention. Very soon the company had a commercial gas-producing plant on the market, based on Murdock's horizontal retort in which the coal was carbonised, burned and vaporised. This remarkably useful by-product of the exploitation of coal transformed both industrial and domestic power consumption in Britain, and until the last quarter of the 20th century 'coal' or 'town' gas was produced in urban centres throughout the country. At the same time, almost one fifth of Britain's entire resources of coal was being consumed in gasworks. Consumption doubled between nationalisation in 1948 and the transfer to natural gas in 1973, a change that further transformed the country's use of – and attitudes to – power.

Local Gasworks

The first company to sell gas from a central generating station through a mains system to independent consumers – the Gas Light & Coke Company – was established in 1812. By 1815 the company had built 26 miles (42km) of underground mains in London. There were more than 1,000 gasworks in Britain by 1900, some being parts of large industrial concerns. In the first half of the 20th century, most of these came under municipal control and exemplified the most positive features of power provision by local authorities. A good example was Birmingham, where the offices of the city gasworks now form part of its art gallery. Following nationalisation in 1948 municipal production centres were taken over by regional supply companies (see p. 31) and the transfer to natural gas meant that all had closed by the late 1970s. The largest gasworks to be built in Britain was at Beckton in London in 1869. In the early 21st century the site was taken over by the eastern terminus of the Docklands Light Railway and its former waste tip was converted into an artificial ski slope.

Gas Holders

🔲 Following its distillation from coal, town gas was stored in enormous steel-framed, iron-plated storage containers, or 'gas holders' (commonly misnamed 'gasometers') from which it was piped to consumers. A large number of these, some of them built in the late 19th century, survived until the last quarter of the 20th, from which time they were gradually replaced

Gas Holder

by underground storage (see below). Their distinctive cylindrical shapes were until recently familiar features of urban landscapes throughout Britain. All were scheduled for replacement by 2004, although some examples, such as those at King's Cross, Battersea and the Oval cricket ground in London, were retained as landmark features.

Gas Boards

🔲 Initially gas was supplied to consumers from individual plants, which in time all came under municipal supervision. The nationalisation of the utilities in 1948 brought the country's 1,000 or so gasworks under the control of 12 area boards. At the same time the industry was rationalised, so that by 1960 the number of gasworks had fallen to a little over 400, while the main system by which networks radiating from individual plants were fed from others outside was greatly extended. The first North Sea gas (see below) was piped ashore at Easington, East Yorkshire, in 1967 and fed through a pipeline to Totley, near Sheffield, from where it was sent down the trunk line supplying Leeds from the south. From this time onwards, the key points in the gas supply industry were the new shore terminals. The modern gas supply system is one based on national and local networks, much of which is hidden, revealed only by occasional signs at the edges of fields marking the course of pipelines below the surface.

Uses of Gas

GAS LIGHTING

The first large-scale street lighting by gas was installed in Pall Mall, London, in January 1807. The effect created on the public imagination by the first reliable public lighting is difficult to exaggerate. Within 10 years of the Gas Light & Coke Company receiving its parliamentary charter in 1812, numerous towns and cities throughout Britain were experiencing the benefits. By the time that interior gas lighting had become common in the 1850s, candles had become a thing of the past. It is sometimes claimed that people's ability to read for longer periods in the day stimulated growth in literacy rates, which itself had an impact in accelerating the rate of industrialisation.

Although the monopoly on street and interior lighting by gas came under threat from electricity in the 1880s, the invention of the incandescent gas mantle in 1885 provided a new lease of life until the mid 20th century, particularly for use at railway stations and in some surviving urban street schemes.

DOMESTIC USES

In the later 19th century, gas became more widely used than just for street lighting with the introduction of the water geyser in

1865, the gas ring in 1867 and the gas fire with radiants in 1880. The greatest expansion of domestic demand came with the wider availability of gas cookers from the 1870s. Gas was not generally used for domestic heating on a substantial scale, however, until the early 20th century.

Natural Gas

In 1959, just as a new terminal for imported liquid gas was being built on Canvey Island in the Thames estuary, a massive field of natural gas was discovered in the Netherlands, suggesting that there was more to be found in the British zone of the North Sea. In the event, the first gas was brought up at the mouth of the Humber in 1965 and the swift adoption of this cleaner source of fuel led to a rapid decline in the use of coal. Conversion to natural gas almost completely eliminated the regional gasworks, of which there were few remaining by the last quarter of the 20th century. As well as general domestic and industrial use, North Sea gas is also utilised for the production of ammonia, methane and hydrogen for a range of industrial applications.

OIL

Coal's near monopoly position as Britain's main source of fuel did not come under threat until the Admiralty's decision in 1914 that the Royal Navy's ships should burn oil rather than coal. Shortly afterwards the British Government took a substantial share in the Anglo Persian Oil Co. At the same time the rapid development of motor transport led to improved refining techniques, and by the second half of the 20th century oil in the form of petroleum distillate was of crucial importance to Britain as to all the advanced economies. So too were the myriad products made from plastics – from clothing to computers – which meant that the global economy of the late 20th century was almost entirely dependent on oil and its by-products.

Oil Refineries

From the 1920s, crude oil supplied by the Anglo Persian Oil Co. was treated at refineries in Britain, like those established by Shell at Shell Haven (Essex), Stanlow (Cheshire) and Ardrossan (Ayrshire). Refineries were also built at Ellesmere Port (Cheshire) and Trafford Park, Manchester, the latter being used mainly for lubricating oils, as was a plant at Stanlow built for the RAF, which began operation in 1940. The refining side of the industry was transformed after the Second World War, partly owing to the increased demand for motor fuel but also because refineries became the principal suppliers of feed stocks to the chemical industry.

During the inter-war period, Stanlow was gradually enlarged and absorbed several other oil installations in the Ellesmere Port area. Further large-scale developments took place on the Tees in the vicinity of Middlesbrough in the late 1960s and early 1970s. As aspects of industrial heritage, oil refineries have received little attention, mainly because the processes carried on within them – if quite unspectacular compared to the processing of metals – are generally not well understood. However, this is a situation that is likely to change since oil refineries were some of the most important industrial sites established in the 20th century and the source of many of the products that have shaped our daily lives.

North Sea Oil Terminals

Like gas, the oil industry underwent significant changes following the discovery of reserves under the North Sea in the

1960s and in Morecambe Bay in the mid 1970s. At the production end of the industry, oil platforms are rarely seen other than by workers in the industry themselves, but are, nevertheless, remarkable engineering achievements in their own right. Even the principal terminals with their massive cylindrical tanks and discharge gantries, such as those at Sullom Voe in Shetland and Popton Point in Pembrokeshire, are away from main centres of population. However, a number of the traditional fishing ports of eastern Britain such as Aberdeen, Great Yarmouth and Lowestoft were transformed in the later 20th century as fish stocks declined and facilities were given over instead to servicing the North Sea oil industry.

CHAPTER TWO

MATERIALS

More than anything, the Industrial Revolution witnessed dramatic developments in the production and use of both natural and synthetic materials. The significance of these developments is that they enabled a huge leap to take place in the scale of human endeavour. From the iron that went into steam engines, to steel-hulled ships and oil-fuelled airliners, the revolution in use of materials was the springboard to a world that, within less than 200 years, was to change beyond all recognition.

IRON AND STEEL

If coal was the quintessential fuel of the Industrial Revolution, iron was its material essence. The working of iron, and its alloy derivative steel, was one of the defining processes of industrialisation and is still, in the early 21st century, at the core of Britain's material culture. For nearly

200 years Britain led the way in technological developments, and the iron industry which was born in the wooded valleys of Shropshire, was at the root of the subsequent spread of industrialisation throughout much of the world. Symbolic of the intimate relationship between metalwork and technology in this period is the fact that the great genius of mechanical engineering, Thomas Newcomen, started out himself as an ironmonger.

A crucial first step in the development of ironworking from a small-scale, localised industrial activity to one that literally changed the world was the replacement of charcoal with purified coal – coke – as the main fuel in iron smelting. It is no exaggeration to say that the coke smelting process perfected at Coalbrookdale in Shropshire by Abraham Darby in 1709 was one of the main technological breakthroughs of the industrial period. Until this time the high sulphur content in coal had rendered iron too brittle for anything other than relatively small-scale applications, such as hand tools and weapons. Apart from the technological considerations, the development of the coke smelting process was also precipitated by the enactment of laws to preserve timber supplies for naval shipbuilding. Significant as the discovery of the process of coke manufacture was, however, it was a process very similar to the production of charcoal which had preceded it. Essentially, this consisted of burning coal in mounds, which starved it of oxygen, thereby releasing its volatile impure components. A more radical change to the area's traditional iron industry came in 1742 when Abraham Darby II installed a Newcomen engine to drive the bellows at his father's forge. It was from this point that progress in the scale of production truly accelerated.

By the late 18th century the intimate connection between fuel, materials and technology that was characteristic of the Industrial Revolution was evident in the Coalbrookdale valley. The need to transport great quantities of coal to be converted to coke and used in the valley's forges led to the development of the railway systems which the Darbys built to connect the coal-mines to their ironworks. This in turn provided impetus to the local iron-masters to produce the first iron rails, wheels and engine cylinders that were such vital components in the spread of indus-trialisation. Such was the fame of Coalbrookdale that it became the centre of the world's first industrial tourism, with visitors coming from all over the world to marvel at, and learn from, the developing new technologies.

Geographical Distribution

The geographical distribution of the iron industry is a reflec-tion of that remarkable geological coincidence that was such a significant contributory factor to Britain's early industrial devel-opment and subsequent rise to economic prominence. In the same series of stratification, and often very near the surface, iron-stone and good-quality coal were available for metalworking, frequently also in combination with the limestone and clay required for construction of furnaces. The area of Coalbrookdale in Shropshire was particularly favoured since the coal lying just below its surface – known as clod coal – was relatively pure in its natural state, a fortunate occurrence that had favoured the devel-opment of iron production in the valley since the 16th century. When Abraham Darby made the decision to relocate his oper-ations from Bristol to Coalbrookdale in 1708, he arrived therefore in a part of the country well supplied with the raw materials for industrial ironworking.

Similar coal measures occurred also in the regions of South Staffordshire, South and West Yorkshire and South Wales – all areas that developed as early centres of ironworking on an industrial scale. Once coke smelting began to overtake the old methods using charcoal, traditional centres of the industry, such as the Wealden areas in the south of England, declined. Other areas with local coal reserves that rose in their place included the Forest of Dean in the West of England, the border area of Shropshire, the Lake District and lowland Scotland.

Another area situated on seams of relatively pure coal – known locally as Staffordshire thick coal – was one that was to become virtually synonymous with industry, the so-called Black Country of the West Midlands. The name appears to date from the middle of the 19th century, when thousands of furnaces and chimneys filled the air with belching black smoke, and the mining of coal, ironstone, fire clay and limestone led to the deterioration of much of the landscape. Another industrial centre that rose to prominence with the rapid development of its traditional metalworking prowess was the South Yorkshire town of Sheffield. The main factor here – in addition to the local availability of iron ore, charcoal supplies and high-quality stone for construction and use as grindstones – was the fast-flowing rivers and streams of its many valleys which provided the power to its growing number of forges.

Once ironworking began to take place on an industrial scale, the chief areas of iron ore extraction were the Cleveland Hills of North Yorkshire, the East Midlands and the hematite areas of North West England. In the Cleveland Hills large-scale mining of iron ore commenced in 1836, and output reached a peak some 50 years later. The greater part of the iron ore used in the blast furnaces of Britain (p. 50) during the 20th century came from the substantial Jurassic deposits of Oxfordshire, Northamptonshire, Rutland, Leicestershire and Lincolnshire, whose landscapes still bear witness to the quarrying of ore on an industrial scale. Up until the outbreak of the

Second World War annual output stood at between 10 and 15 million tonnes, and for much of this time a large part of the country's transport resources were dedicated to the movement of iron ore and coal from the mines and quarries to the blast furnaces of Britain.

Wrought Iron

⊠ The basic principle by which iron is produced is by the removal of oxygen from iron ore by reduction, and then carbon in the form of charcoal or coke combining with the oxygen to release metallic iron. Traditionally, iron ore was heated in a charcoal fire until it took the form of a spongy lump or 'bloom'. In this state it was not molten but could be hammered in order to make tools or weapons, the hammering or 'forging' being fundamental also to the removal of impurities from the metal. The end result was a tough and fibrous material, strong yet easily worked and known as 'wrought iron'.

IRON FORGES

The earliest type of forge was known as a 'bloomery' and had alternating layers of charcoal and iron ore through which air from the manually operated bellows provided sufficient heat for the oxygen in the iron ore to combine with the carbon in the charcoal. The resulting 'bloom' consisted of almost pure iron with a fairly low carbon content, high tensile strength and resistance to corrosion. As demand

Iron Forge

for wrought iron increased, the basic technique developed into two separate stages known as the 'finery' and 'chafery'. The finery was a charcoal hearth in which iron was stirred at high temperature under a blast of air from the bellows. It was at this stage that oxygen in the blast combined first with the silicon and then the carbon, resulting eventually in the spongy mass of iron that formed in the hearth. This was hammered into a rectangular block before being transferred to the chafery. Here it was simply heated to forging temperature so that it could be fashioned into the shape required. The common name for the finery and its associated equipment, the most important being the hammer, was a forge.

INDUSTRIAL USES OF WROUGHT IRON

The significance of wrought iron to engineering began around 1725, when wrought-iron plates started being used instead of copper in the manufacture of steam engine boilers. From that time on its range of applications steadily increased, receiving a further impetus when the Royal Navy started ordering wrought-iron chains to replace the traditional anchor rope. In the mid 1820s the first rolled-iron rails were made for the new railways [see rolling mills, p. 50], and by the 1840s wrought-iron plate was being employed in large-scale engineering projects such as the construction of Brunel's steamship *Great Britain* and Robert Stephenson's tubular Britannia bridge, the latter being followed by a long succession of wrought-iron bridges. The mid-19th-century heyday of engineering in wrought iron culminated in its use in the roof of the massive train shed at St Pancras station, London, in 1868. The manufacture of the first wrought-iron girders commenced a revolution in the construction industry which lasted until their replacement by steel in the second half of the 20th century.

Cast Iron

⊠ The discovery of cast iron was probably made originally through the accidental overheating of material in a bloomery furnace. Once the technique had been perfected, molten iron was run off into a sand pit in which there was a central depression called a 'sow'. There were also side branches leading off from this, inevitably known as 'pigs', and the bars of iron that these formed were known as 'pig iron'. In this form, iron could not be shaped by hammering, and originally its hard brittle nature suggested no obvious uses. However, from the process of being melted, iron in this form has a high carbon content and crystalline structure, which resulted in it being weak in tension but very strong in compression.

IRON BRIDGES AND OTHER IRON STRUCTURES

It was soon realised that the production then melting of bars of cast iron could provide a short-cut to larger quantities of good-quality wrought iron. This, in essence, was the origin of the iron smelting industry based on the charcoal-fuelled blast furnace. From the 1720s, ironworks in Coalbrookdale had been casting cylinders for Newcomen engines in iron instead of the traditional brass, and the region reached the peak of its fame for use of this material with the building of the iron bridge – the first in the world – in 1779. The individual members for this revolutionary structure were cast by John 'Iron Mad' Wilkinson nearby in the valley, which before long was receiving a steady stream of tourists who came to gaze at it in wonder. By the end of the 18th century cast iron was well on the way to acceptance as an important material for use in engineering, with applications including steam engines, support columns and beams for factories, mills and warehouses, bridges and aqueducts, as well as a myriad of components for machines of all types and sizes.

Steel

🎯 Steel is essentially an alloy of iron and carbon, with a lower carbon content than cast iron but greater than wrought iron. From an early stage in the history of ironworking, it was realised that the carbon content influenced the ability of the metal to take a sharpened edge and, for this reason, small quantities of steel were widely produced for providing an edge to swords and tips for arrowheads. These early processes consisted of heating pure wrought iron in contact with charcoal in a hearth, so that it would absorb carbon.

The first successful attempts at producing large quantities of steel came with the invention of the cementation furnace in the early 17th century. By this method wrought iron was given a higher carbon content by sealing it in fired clay pots with a carbon-rich mixture provided mainly by charcoal. Since oxygen was not admitted, some of the charcoal impregnated the surface of the iron bars, converting it to steel. The resulting material was then heated using a coal-fired reverberatory cementation furnace, the product of which was known as 'blister-steel' on account of its surface appearance.

SHEAR STEEL

This early steel tended to be of rather poor quality and inconsistent structure. Better quality was achieved by binding a number of iron bars into what was called a 'faggot', which was then forged and welded to produce so-called 'shear steel' on account of its application in making cutting tools. In the last decades of the 17th century high-quality Swedish iron started to be imported to north-eastern England for conversion to steel, and a number of cementation furnaces became established in the vicinity of Newcastle upon Tyne.

CRUCIBLE STEEL

A major technological revolution occurred in 1740 when Benjamin Huntsman (1704–76), a clockmaker from Doncaster, introduced the crucible method of making steel from bar or blister steel, originally for the purpose of making more uniform steel for springs and pendulums. This significant breakthrough allowed impurities in the metal to float to the surface and be skimmed off under intense heat produced by burning coke. The resulting liquid steel was then poured into a mould and allowed to solidify, producing an ingot of cast or 'crucible' steel with a uniformly high degree of purity. By perfecting this method, Huntsman effectively laid the foundation for the development of the steel industry not just in Sheffield, where he worked, but the entire world. A good example of the layout of a crucible steelworks can be seen at the Abbeydale industrial hamlet on the outskirts of Sheffield.

MILD STEEL AND THE BESSEMER CONVERTER

The problem with crucible steel was that it could not be produced cheaply in bulk. It was a problem overcome in 1856 by Henry Bessemer (1812–98), whose apparatus, known as the Bessemer converter, though unable to produce steel of the same quality, could produce it in much higher quantity. The process that he developed was relatively simple. A trunnion-mounted container with a perforated bottom through which air was blown was tipped up to receive a charge of molten pig iron. It was then returned to the upright position and had air blown through

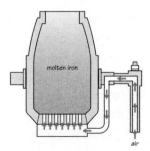

Bessemer Converter

the holes, which had the effect of oxidising the carbon, silica and manganese within the iron. When the process was complete, as judged by the material's colour, the blast of air was reduced and additions were made in order to achieve the desired alloy on that particular occasion. The steel was then poured off into a ladle and then into ingot moulds. The material produced by the Bessemer conversion process was known as 'mild steel' and came largely to replace wrought iron as an engineering material since the former could not be made in such great quantities. Within 15 years of the development of this method, large quantities of steel were being used for making rails, boiler plate, and in shipbuilding, and the second half of the 19th century witnessed a commensurate decline in the output of wrought iron.

OPEN-HEARTH FURNACES

The final significant phase in the development of the steel industry in the 19th century was the introduction of the regenerative open-hearth furnace by C.W. Siemens (1823–83), which used ore to assist in oxidising the excess carbon and other impurities produced when pig iron was converted to steel. Until the end of the 19th century the carbon steel produced by these processes was all that was available. However, it was gradually discovered that carbon steel could be improved by adding other elements, and the history of steel making in the 20th century was essentially one of an increasingly sophisti-

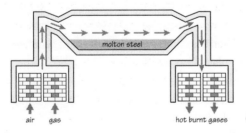

Open-Hearth Furnace

cated development of alloy steels. Most of the greatest contributions in this regard occurred in Sheffield, the traditional home of iron and steel making. A significant milestone was reached in 1882 with Robert Hadfield's first production of manganese steel, an extremely hard-wearing material which was ideal for railway and tram lines. Silicon steel, also discovered by Hadfield, was found to have magnetic properties greater than iron itself and was soon adopted commercially for making electromagnetic equipment such as that used in the transformers of electrical generating equipment.

STAINLESS STEEL

The most important discovery in the field of alloy steels was made in 1913 when Henry Brierley perfected the production of stainless steel, which was to revolutionise the cutlery industry. The rest of the 20th century witnessed the development of a whole host of specialised alloy steels, which, together, have transformed the face of engineering.

Uses of Steel

ARMAMENTS

The rise to dominance of steel as the paramount industrial material can be seen most readily in the development of Sheffield; over the course of the period it went from being the country's prime producer of cutlery and tools to one of the greatest industrial and engineering centres in the world. Not for the last time, developments in the armaments industry stimulated the rate of change in industry as a whole. When the company of John Brown manufactured the first armour plate at its Sheffield works in 1861, other companies soon followed. By 1914 the huge works owned by companies such as Vickers, Cammell, Firth and Brown had made Sheffield the centre of the world's armaments industry.

CONSTRUCTION

As well as armaments, the future of steel was to be in construction, but it was not until the early 20th century that the material was accepted as suitable for large-scale projects. The completion of the Forth Rail Bridge in 1890 showed the way, itself taking the lead from the ambitious Brooklyn Bridge built in New York in 1883. By the 1880s, steel girders had become widely adopted for large-scale building works, such as the Great Northern Railway warehouse in Manchester, built to a revolutionary design incorporating a riveted steel frame (see p. 89).

COMMERCIAL USAGE

During the First World War steel was widely used in the construction of aircraft factories and hangars. However, one of the most rapid developments in the use of steel was in the manufacture of a more humble product. Tinplate – steel rolled thin and coated with tin – was used for canning of foodstuffs, itself a major contributor to the convenience culture of the industrial world. Over the course of the 20th century steel was to go on to become one of the most influential modern materials, and as production methods improved it became unrivalled for low cost and adaptability.

Forges and Rolling Mills

As stated earlier, the most important invention contributing to the development of the industrial-scale forge was the water-powered tilt hammer, which paved the way for the mass production of steel. Using tilt hammers, bundles or 'faggots' of blister steel bars could be forge-welded and the mass of carbon-impregnated iron could then be drawn out under the tilt hammer to form bars of 'shear' steel. Further improvements to the quality of the end-product could be made simply by repeating the process, such as in making bars of 'double shear steel' in which the carbon was more evenly distributed. Water-powered tilt hammers of the kind that became common in the river valleys of Sheffield enabled the manufacture of large edge tools such as scythes. The operation of tilt hammers is described on p. 9; often the only remaining evidence of their former presence in the landscape is in the form of the 'hammer ponds' that once provided the head of water vital for the power of the water wheel.

HYDRAULIC FORGE

As the rate of technological change increased rapidly after the first quarter of the 19th century, there was a require-ment for ever larger pieces of steel. However, there was a limit to the size of jobs that could be taken on by the tradi-tional tilt hammer. This situation was addressed in 1839 when James Naysmith invented the steam hammer, which was both sent down

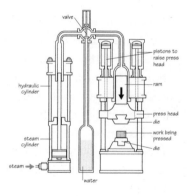

Hydraulic Forging Press

with great force and lifted up again using the power of steam. A further improvement in steel production came with the intro-duction of the hydraulic forging press by Charles Cammell at his Sheffield works in 1863. Unlike the traditional hammer, the press squeezed the steel into shape, enabling larger and more complex pieces to be produced to satisfy the increasingly rigor-ous demands of engineering.

ROLLING MILL

A parallel development in steel forging was the rolling mill, invented by Henry Cort in 1783 to meet the needs of the Sheffield tool and cutlery industries for steel in small rods. Under Cort's system, large pieces of hot steel were passed between grooved rolls, gradually reducing it in size. The steel was moved about by hand

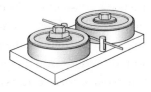

Rolling Mill

between the rolls, a process known as 'hand rolling'. Depending on the shape of the grooves that were selected for any particular job, iron could be produced in round or square section. By the end of the 18th century, the combination of the puddling furnace (see p. 52) and grooved rolls led to a huge increase in the output of wrought iron.

Furnaces

BLAST FURNACES

Since the 15th century the main source of heat used in iron-working has been that known as the 'blast furnace', which enabled larger quantities of iron to be produced than in the traditional bloomeries. As we have seen, cast iron from the furnace was run off into depressions in a bed of sand, the main runner of which was called the sow and the side branches 'pigs'. Unlike the bloomeries that preceded them, the air supply for blast furnaces usually came from bellows, although the greater energy required meant that they were typically powered by water wheels. Once the rough bars of brittle cast iron had cooled, they were sent to forges for working into wrought iron.

For reasons of efficiency, early blast furnaces typically carried on smelting throughout the night, and therefore needed a constant supply of raw materials in the form of iron ore, wood for charcoal, water to power the bellows, and limestone and clay to build the furnace. A typical blast furnace site would be built into a slope or hillside, often the side of a watercourse, with an access bank or bridge for introducing the raw materials, a process known as 'charging'. The blast furnaces of the Forest of Dean were some of the earliest in Britain to be charged from above. At the foot of the slope there needed to be room for the pig bed, often protected from the elements by a 'casting shed', which might also contain the bellows.

CUPOLAS AND BOX BELLOWS

The full potential of coke smelting over charcoal would remain out of reach until a stronger blast of air could be supplied than was available from traditional water bellows. Progress came in the form of the box bellows and 'cupolas' introduced in the late 1750s. The most significant technological improvement, however, was James Watt's steam blowing engine of 1775, which brought the added bonus of freeing the blast furnace process from the requirement of being sited next to running streams. Much evidence of this crucial period in the development of iron making can be seen in the Coalbrookdale area of Shropshire. The cupola was an alternative to the traditional air furnace and took the form of a shaft in which coke was burnt and brought to high heat by air blown through a system of pipes. It was first patented by the ironmaster John Wilkinson in 1794, and an early example is preserved at the Ironbridge Gorge Museum.

PUDDLING FURNACE

A significant innovation was the puddling furnace introduced in 1784 by Henry Cort (1740–1800), which worked by stirring molten pig iron until it was converted into malleable iron. During the process, contact between the molten metal and the coal that was used as fuel was avoided, thereby dispensing with the need for blowing machinery.

HOT BLAST FURNACE

In 1828 Scottish ironworkers developed the hot blast furnace, which allowed smelting to take place at higher temperature and at the same time meant that coke could be replaced by ordinary coal as fuel.

By 1900 there were around 600 blast furnaces in Britain, mostly sited on or near to the main coalfields. By the time of the outbreak of the First World War, technological improvements had led to a huge increase in both output and demand for iron. Evidence of this is the vast Templeborough works, built near Rotherham in South Yorkshire, in which there was space for 14 open-hearth furnaces to operate simultaneously. In the 1960s the plant was modified in order to accommodate 600-ton electric arc furnaces, the state-of-the-art technology of the later 20th century. By this time electric air blowers and automatic charging of raw material had both become standard.

As the capacity of individual plants was expanded, the number of blast furnaces around the country diminished, and at the end of the 20th century there were just 15 furnaces in operation at four giant steelworks at Margam, Llanwern, Scunthorpe and Redcar. In stark contrast to the integration of raw material and finished product that was witnessed at the start of industrial ironworking, these later plants were entirely dependent on imported iron ore and coal.

TIN

Tin mining has a long history in Britain, going back to the Bronze Age when tin was a major export. Its earliest use was mainly in an alloy with copper to form bronze for tools and weapons, and later as 'bell metal'. Later still, alloyed with lead, it was used to produce pewter for domestic utensils and solder for general metalworking purposes. After iron, tin ore has probably been the most extensively worked metal-bearing mineral in the country, with the world-renowned Cornish tin mining industry reaching its peak in the second half of the 19th century.

Geographical Distribution

Although tin has been mined in various parts of Britain, the most extensive remains of the industry are in the Cornish peninsula, the prime producing area for the metal in Europe for some 2,000 years. From the late 19th century onwards, the local industry came under pressure from imports, in particular from Malaysia, and was all but extinct by the early 20th century. However, a steep increase in the price of metals in the early 21st century – mainly a response to increased production of technologically based products, particularly in China – has opened up the possibility of some recovery.

At the peak of production in the mid 19th century a sizeable quantity of the tin mined in Cornwall was transported across the Bristol Channel to tinplate works situated near to the South Wales coalfields. Tinplate manufacture had been established in the vicinity of Pontypool and Kidwelly in the early 18th century, and the industry continued to flourish, albeit with steel replacing the original wrought iron, until the second half of the 20th century.

Tin Mining

The main problem encountered in the industrial mining of tin was drainage, which was especially problematic in Cornwall where coal was expensive owing to lack of local supplies. The answer came in the development of the efficient Boulton & Watt steam engines (see p. 21), which, since they used less than one third of the coal consumed by the original Newcomen engines, were an immediate success. A specialist variation was the Cornish pump engine developed by Richard Trevithick from a prototype erected in 1812 at the Wheal Prosper tin mine at Gwithian in Cornwall. These machines operated at a much higher pressure than the Boulton & Watt engines, and used a system known as expansive working to gain extra efficiency. The Cornish beam engine had a single-acting apparatus whereby the steam operated pump rods in the mine shaft. As a result of their popularity, one of the most distinctive heritage features of Cornwall and, to a lesser extent Devon, are the engine houses of which up to a few hundred still survive. Easily recognisable in the landscape, the typical Cornish engine house is a rectangular stone-built structure with a round chimney in one corner opposite a massive 'bob wall' on which the engine beam was able to rock.

COPPER

Copper was one of the earliest metals to be worked, but it was not until it was alloyed with tin to form bronze that it came to be widely used in the form of tools, weapons and coinage. Industrialisation found new uses for the metal, such as in coating the hulls of wooden sailing ships and making boilers for the ubiquitous steam engines. However, the greatest leap in demand for copper during the Industrial Revolution was as brass, its alloy with zinc. Demand for brass grew rapidly in the metal trades, and among engine and machine manufacturers, and was a leading factor in the dramatic growth of Birmingham as an industrial centre from the later 18th century. Mining, quarrying and smelting of copper all expanded on a massive scale from the late 18th century until decline set in during the 1870s following the opening of the massive Rio Tinto mines in Spain.

Geographical Distribution

The main centres of the British copper industry were in Cornwall, North Wales (including Anglesey), Devon and the Lake District. As with other metals, the smelting of copper required coal, and smelting works therefore tended to concentrate around coalfield locations. By the 1720s copper smelting had moved from the Cornish copper mines across the Bristol Channel to Swansea, where coal could be obtained for half the price. This was especially significant since greater quantities of fuel were consumed than ore during the smelting process. The copper mined at Anglesey, where the Parys Mountain site became one of the largest copper mines in the world, was smelted mainly in the region of the Lancashire coalfield, and was a contributory factor in the industrial growth of St Helens. At the height of the copper industry in the mid 19th century it had become a highly integrated process, with the main companies in control of all of the various stages.

Copper Mining, Processing and Distribution

Some of the most extensive remains of the copper mining industry are to be found in the Coniston area of the English Lake District, where the industry developed in the early 1830s. Processing of the copper ore was very labour intensive and at its peak in the 1850s employed some 600 people, including women and children. Power was supplied by the abundant fast-flowing streams in the area, of which 13 were in use in the mid 19th century. Originally, the ore was taken on tram tracks to be shipped from the harbour at Greenodd at the rate of about 250 tons a month. From 1859 onwards the extension of the rail network meant that the material could be transported more efficiently still.

In Coniston and elsewhere, decline set into the industry soon after the Rio Tinto mines started full-scale production in 1873, and was hastened by additional competition from Chile in the early 1880s. Until that point, and particularly between 1700 and 1870, copper had been of great importance to the Cornish economy, with a number of sites mining both copper and tin concurrently. However, probably the most spectacular of all the copper mining sites in Britain was Parys Mountain in Anglesey, which began as a series of small mines in the late 1760s but developed into a vast open-cast quarry.

LEAD

Lead had been mined in Britain from at least as early as the Roman period, but the main rise in demand came in the middle of the 19th century, when the huge growth in population that occurred with industrialisation called for massive quantities to be used in plumbing and roofing. Employed industrially from the earlier 18th century in the manufacture of boilers for steam engines, lead came increasingly to be used as an additive to industrial compounds such as paints. The industry was severely hit by the increasing scale of imports of foreign ores, which occurred from around 1900, and by the middle of the 20th century was in terminal decline. However, some smelting and processing of lead, using foreign ore, did continue in Britain.

Geographical Distribution and Methods of Lead Mining

LIBERTIES

The traditional centres of lead mining before the Industrial Revolution had been the Derbyshire Peak District and Somerset. Both of these were organised according to working areas known as 'liberties', within which miners were free to sink pits on the condition of paying regular dues in relation to their output. The miners tended to work in groups of between four and six men, and every three months would make their 'bargain' with the mine agent, by which the rate was set for their next period of work. The earliest lead workings took the form of shallow pits, which followed the long veins of ore. Over each pit a timber winch would be mounted by which buckets of ore were wound up the shaft. Once each successive pit had been worked out another shaft would be sunk further along the vein so that today former lead working districts can be identified by the lines of abandoned shafts marking the course of worked-out veins in the landscape.

WATER GATES

As with coal, the scale of early lead mining activities was limited by difficulties in drainage. To a certain extent these were overcome quite effectively by systems of underground ditches and tunnels known in the North East of England as 'water gates', in

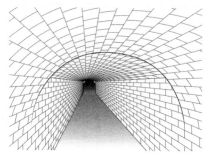

Sough

the south as 'adits' and in much of the Midlands, including the extensive lead mining area of the Derbyshire Peak District, as 'soughs'. However, these were unable to cope with the demands of deep working, and it was not until the introduction of steam pumping engines in about 1712 that mining was able to take place at greater depth. In the North Pennines, in particular, adits continued to be used, often enlarged and known as 'horse levels', through which ponies could haul tubs of ore out of the mine. The entrances of many of these tunnels can still be seen in the landscape of the area today.

OPEN-CAST LEAD WORKING

By the 18th century large-scale open-cast working of lead was also carried out, using water power to remove the overlying earth known as 'overburden'. This involved the construction of an earthwork dam on the hillside above the lead vein. Once the surface ground had been loosened below the dam, a torrent of water was released which, together with the occasional use of gunpowder, broke up the ore-bearing rock below the surface. Continued repetition of this process, known as 'hushing', produced an artificial valley along the lead vein, from which workers were able simply to pick out the lead ore that gathered at the bottom of the 'hush'.

The increase in demand for the metal during the 19th century led to migration of activities to the North Pennines, which, despite the continued importance of Derbyshire in particular, became the main producing area. At its height in the mid 19th century the mining and processing of lead ore employed hundreds of adult and child workers in the remote valleys of the region. Other areas which saw a growth in lead mining activity included Northumberland, County Durham, North Wales and Shropshire. As in the case of tin and copper, there was an increasing movement of the smelting process towards coalfield locations.

ALUMINIUM

In the late 19th century aluminium – an elemental metal of low density, resistant to corrosion and with high electrical and thermal conduction properties – was first used industrially in the manufacture of domestic utensils and toothpaste tubes. From the 1930s, on account of its properties, it became an essential material in aircraft construction. Its wider use, however, came under increasing competition from special steels and plastics. The metal is obtained by reduction of aluminium oxide, itself derived from bauxite. The process demands electric power in huge quantities, and so aluminium smelting plants are typically situated next to hydroelectric power stations in the highland zone of Britain (see p. 72).

CHEMICALS

Although it can be difficult nowadays to make a clear distinction between the chemical and oil industries (see p. 61), some British chemical companies, not directly connected to oil, are among the longest established industrial concerns in the country. Some of the earliest chemical companies made products based on coal and its derivatives as well as organic materials such as molasses. Even in the mid 20th century, many British chemical works still contained rows of coke ovens and used wood pulp and molasses as chief ingredients in their processes.

One of the earliest British chemical companies, Albright &Wilson, developed from a phosphorus match works set up in the 1830s and went on to produce a variety of industrial compounds. By the 20th century, chemicals were of fundamental importance to the national economy and had changed the face of British industry. Following the depression of the 1930s, there was large-scale investment in chemical works such as that at

Billingham in Cheshire, and the most significant company of this period, Imperial Chemical Industries (ICI), greatly expanded its operations during the Second World War. Owing to the apparently specialist nature of many of its processes, however, the chemical industry has been generally neglected by historians.

Geographical Distribution of the Chemical Industry

◉ The industrial chemical concern established by John Brunner and Ludwig Mond in the 1870s in Cheshire formed the nucleus of what remained one of the chief concentrations of chemical manufacture in Britain until the end of the 20th century. The best known of these subsequent chemical works is the ICI plant at Winnington. Other concentrations of chemical plants include Billingham and Wilton on Teesside, Stanlow, Runcorn and Widnes on the Mersey estuary, Llandarcy and Baglan Bay near Swansea, Immingham on the Humber estuary and Grangemouth on the Forth. These sites include some of the most striking industrial landscapes in Britain and reflect the fundamental significance of chemicals to the modern British industrial scene.

Chemical Plants

◉ Not only have historians and industrial archaeologists generally neglected chemical plants, since they cannot be easily adapted to new uses in the same way as, say, disused textile mills or warehouses, neither have they been so easily assimilated into the public consciousness. However, many sites have remained in use for a century or more and some of the basic structures still visible in chemical plants were originally designed in the first decade of the 20th century.

One of those with a long history is the Billingham site on Teesside, which within 10 years of its establishment in 1920 had become a closely packed rectangular complex in the middle of a road and railway system further subdivided by a network of pipelines. Half of the site was taken up by the tall steel-framed sheds of the ammonia plant, itself flanked by boilers, workshops and stores. On the other side of the main pipelines were two sulphate plants and the vast storage silo. Next to this was a water gas plant built for generating the gases used in synthesis of ammonia, and a number of coke ovens.

Together, Billingham and Wilton marked a high point of confidence in the possibilities for large-scale, high-technology industry in Britain. Up until the 1970s they formed Europe's largest petrochemical complex, and in contrast to current sensibilities, the visual aspects of the sites were advertised with pride. At its height in the late 1950s, Billingham employed about 17,000 people and there were about 13,000 at Wilton 10 years later. Both sites are now much reduced in scale.

Petrochemicals and Plastics

▣ The first investment in what is now known as the petrochemical industry occurred at the time of a slump in demand for fertilisers in the 1930s and took the form of the construction of plant for the hydrogenation of coal and creosote into petrol. In the 1950s the production of petrol by this method became less economical, and so plant was adapted to produce phenol and isopropanol for use in plastics, and later to produce detergent alcohols used in washing-up liquids and other cleaning agents.

PETROCHEMICAL PLANTS
The first petrochemical plant in Britain was probably that established at Carrington near Manchester in the early 1960s using oil

from the Stanlow refinery on the Wirral. But it was the construction of the Wilton plant by ICI that marked the recognition that the future of the chemical industry would be based on oil. The first processing furnace at Wilton started production in 1951 and by the late 1950s there were five tall cylindrical processing units (known as 'steam crackers') on site, forming the most distinctive feature of the plant. The example of ICI was followed by other companies in the second half of the 20th century, and the majority of chemical plants are now situated next to the main oil refineries at Fawley (Hampshire), Baglan Bay, Stanlow and Grangemouth.

PLASTICS INDUSTRY
Despite the ubiquitous nature of its products, the associated plastics industry that developed in the 20th century is another that has been largely neglected. In the industrial and manufacturing context, plastics can be defined as materials containing long chains of carbon atoms, which in combination with oxygen, hydrogen and other atoms can be shaped without losing their cohesion. The industrial production of natural plastics such as shellac and bitumen, used originally as stoppers for beer bottles, goes back to the 19th century, and the technology of plastics production advanced rapidly during the First World War.

CONCRETE

Although concrete – a cement matrix with an aggregate of stones and sand – is often regarded as an entirely modern constructional material, it was first used by the Romans in bridges, aqueducts and other large-scale public engineering works. In modern times, concrete was first used in Britain in mass form – that is, without reinforcement – in the construction of London docks in the early 19th century. Such material continued to be used occasionally in construction works such as foundations, sea walls and breakwaters, but it was not until the 1820s that the first attempts were made to produce and utilise concrete industrially. In particular, the massive increase in large-scale engineering works at this time produced a demand not only for ordinary cement, but so-called hydraulic materials, which could set in the absence of air and thus be used in the foundations of bridges and aqueducts.

PORTLAND CEMENT

The first stage in this process came with the invention in 1824 of Portland cement – so called because it was used initially to imitate Portland stone – which was made by the combined combustion of limestone and clay. From the 1850s, Portland cement was used increasingly in place of the traditional lime cements, and its greatly improved strength in turn stimulated experiments in the application of concrete in civil engineering projects and general building work.

Uses of Concrete in Construction

Probably the first concrete bridge in Britain, though built using the mass rather than reinforced concrete technique, was that which crosses the River Axe at Seaton in Devon, dating from the 1880s. Surviving examples of early reinforced concrete structures are rare and often not recognised for what they are. One of the first was the large concrete-framed building situated near the entrance to Bristol docks, while the Free Bridge, which crosses the Severn half a mile (0.8km) downstream from the iconic iron bridge of 1779, was probably one of the first bridges built of reinforced concrete when it was erected in 1908.

The engineering industry became increasingly interested in concrete, because it provided a potentially less expensive method of construction than the steel frame and brick, which had become standard in the second half of the 19th century. At the same time it was more fireproof than brick and so did not need to be encased in tile or plaster. The first concrete floors were installed in textile mills from the 1890s, and by the turn of the century the French

CWS Warehouse

engineers who led the way in use of the new material were building numerous concrete structures in Britain, including warehouses and granaries. The oldest surviving large-scale ferro-concrete building in Britain is probably the Co-operative Wholesale Society (CWS) warehouse at Newcastle upon Tyne, built between 1897 and 1900.

By the end of the 19th century concrete was being used in the construction of some of the last viaducts to be built on British railway lines, the best example being at Glenfinnan on the Mallaig extension of the West Highland Railway, which opened in 1898. This consists of 21 arches each with a span of 50 feet (15m). Technically speaking, the concrete used in this landmark example of late Victorian engineering is not reinforced but formed in timber moulds, though a system of steel plates was incorporated in the centre of the bridge to act against differential movement.

In the first half of the 20th century the use of concrete spread to all types of buildings, and further stimulus was provided to the nascent industry by restrictions on the use of steel during the First World War and also by the need to protect armaments factories from fire and explosion. By 1920 perhaps 90 per cent of multi-storey factories in Britain were constructed using reinforced concrete, an added benefit of which was that it allowed the insertion of large windows. Outstanding examples are the Arrol Johnston car factory near Dumfries and the Birmingham Small Arms (BSA) works in Birmingham.

CHAPTER THREE

MANUFACTURE, PRODUCTION AND DISTRIBUTION

One of the defining features of industrialisation was that it involved new ways of making, distributing and selling things. Primarily, this was a shift away from things being made on a small scale by local people for local markets towards a system where goods were produced in large quantity for more distant markets, often by a labour force drawn from some distance itself. More than anything, it was about where and how people worked.

During the 18th century a great movement of local populations occurred throughout Britain as labour came to be concentrated in single locations. The reason for this was efficiency, and the place where people went came to be known as a 'factory'. Though the factory system which developed during the industrial period is not as pervasive as it once was, its underlying premise – that most of us leave home and go to work as a component of a labour force – is still very much with us.

COTTAGE INDUSTRY

It would be wrong to see the factory system as arriving on the scene fully formed. In fact, in most of its features it developed quite naturally from traditional practice whereby individual householders processed raw materials into finished products to meet their own needs. Since it was to textile working that the factory system was first applied, it is in this area that the evolution of the system can be most easily observed.

Traditionally, individual households within a locality would take the wool sheared from their sheep and process it themselves. This would involve cleaning, 'carding', by which the fibres were separated, spinning of the fibres into a thread or 'yarn' and, finally, weaving this into fabric for making up into an item of clothing. It can be seen, therefore, that there were a number of distinct stages, known as 'processes', involved in turning the raw material into the finished product.

SPINNING-WHEELS AND HAND-LOOMS

Over the years apparatus was devised to facilitate the spinning and weaving processes, the spinning-wheel in the former case and hand-loom in the latter. From the early 18th century local entrepreneurs started to employ spinners and weavers as outworkers, whereby spun yarn or woven textiles were collected from their homes on a regular basis. This mode of production – known as 'cottage industry' – is in essence the transition from household manufacture to the factory system.

Layout of Weavers' Cottages

⌘ Good surviving examples of the type of buildings that developed to meet the needs of cottage industry can be found in the Lancashire parish of Saddleworth in the heart of the Pennine wool country. Essentially this was a development from the traditional arrangement of farm buildings around a central courtyard. The rooms where the families worked were provided with adequate lighting by rows of close-set windows on the upper floors, and at one corner there would be a large, elevated 'taking-in door' accessed by an external staircase, at which raw materials were delivered directly to the work rooms. Similar layouts, particularly with regard to lighting, can be seen in, for example, the silk workers' premises at Macclesfield in Cheshire and at Spitalfields in London. However, though light was needed for workers to be able to see, there was a trade-off as there was less chance of yarn breaking in darker, damp conditions. For this reason, in some weavers' cottages at Newark in Nottinghamshire the main work was performed in sub-surface cellars.

Mechanisation: the Spinning Jenny and the Flying Shuttle

⌘ In terms of premises, then, it can be seen that the arrangement of buildings that met the needs of cottage industry developed quite easily into the later mills and factories of full-blown industrialisation (see p. 82). The other reason that textiles manufacture was at the forefront of developments was that its various processes lent themselves well to mechanisation. The most significant innovations in this regard were the 'spinning jenny' invented by James Hargreaves in 1764 and the improved 'flying shuttle' introduced by William Horrocks in 1813.

The jenny (like 'gin' another corruption of the word 'engine',

Spinning Jenny

meaning 'machine') enabled cotton to be spun on multiple spindles. Early machines had eight spindles, later models 16, so that the amount of yarn that could be produced was increased substantially. The flying shuttle had a similar effect on the rate at which a hand-loom weaver could produce finished cloth.

The natural development from all this increased efficiency was that instead of collecting the finished materials of each stage of production from individual households scattered over the countryside, entrepreneurs began collecting workers at a single site and paying them a weekly wage. From the coming together of multiple-roomed premises and improved machinery, the factory system was born.

WORKSHOPS

Another development from the layout of domestic and agricultural buildings, and one which remained on a small scale, was the workshop. The workshop system developed particularly within areas of manufacturing where it was impossible for a single craftsman to carry out all the processes involved. A good example is the Sheffield hand tool and cutlery trades in which craftsmen would take in blanks (rough unfinished metal shapes) from the forge, fashion them into knives or tools, then pass them on for grinding, polishing and setting of handles.

Workshops were essentially functional buildings, the main requirements of which were a source of heat – usually a hearth or forge – and a reasonably well-lit work area. Most workshops were therefore made of brickwork or stone, in order to withstand heat, and few were given much ornamentation, though exceptions can be found such as the Gothic-arched workshops within the blast furnace complex at Blists Hill, near Ironbridge, or the castellated bottle ovens of some Staffordshire potteries.

The self-contained size of the production unit can be seen well in surviving Black Country chain shops, and the domestic origins of the courtyard arrangement in the restored workshops of Birmingham's jewellery quarter. In the latter case, industrial self-confidence and civic pride prompted local architects in the 1860s to use polychromatic brickwork to create Gothic and Italianate façades.

MILLS

It was the development of water-powered spinning machines that enabled the factory system to really take off. The distinction of being the very first factory may well belong to Thomas Cotchett's three-storey silk spinning mill on the River Derwent in Derby, which opened in 1702. In the event, it ultimately failed as an economic enterprise, but the scale of the operation, its use of complex machinery powered from a single source and the size of its workforce would all tend towards substantiating its claim to be the first. The importance of water power in the earliest factories is attested by the enduring use of the word 'mill', alluding to the fact that they derived their power from the same source as the earlier grinding mills.

The first water-powered cotton spinning mill to be successfully established was that opened up by Thomas Arkwright at Cromford, near Matlock Bath in Derbyshire, in 1771. The dependence on a reliable source of water power meant that most of the early mills were established in rural areas, which meant that scarcity of labour was often a problem. However, as well as being a master of the application of machinery to industrial processes, Arkwright developed a good understanding of the organisation of labour and soon set about encouraging workers to move in from elsewhere and providing for their needs on site (see p. 134).

Geographical Distribution

As long as water power remained the prime consideration in the construction of textile mills, they tended to be situated away from the main centres of habitation and communication networks. The earliest were concentrated in the remote Pennine valleys of Lancashire, Derbyshire and Staffordshire, and within 35 years of the establishment of Cromford the first mills had also been built in central Scotland.

When Arkwright travelled north in 1784 to seek new sites for the development of his industrial system, he found what he was looking for at a point in the upper Clyde valley where the river rushed through a narrow gorge. In such a place Arkwright's new machines, powered by a single giant water wheel, could do the work of thousands of individual spinners. By 1793 four mills had been constructed, and the site, which became known as New Lanark, had become the largest single industrial enterprise in Scotland.

By the early 19th century much of the original Midlands-based textile industry had migrated to Lancashire, partly to avoid the machine-breaking riots of the Luddites which originated in Nottinghamshire, and partly to take advantage of the fact that the damp climate to the west of the Pennines was ideal for the spinning of cotton thread. Once the application of steam power to textile manufacture had liberated mills from the need to be situated next to watercourses, Lancashire's predominance was assured. In the burgeoning town of Manchester the industry had a ready market for its finished product, while the later development of a canal link with Liverpool ensured continuing access to the raw cotton imported from America. The area also had good access to fuel in the form of the coal that powered the steam engines, and to a convenient supply of labour from the growing Lancashire conurbation. An enduring feature of the industrial geography of Britain was thus established.

Machinery and the Use of Power

WATER-POWERED MACHINERY

Application of power to the driving of machinery was one of the main features of the evolution of the factory system during the Industrial Revolution (see p. 10). From the late 18th century, engineers devoted increasing time and energy to improving the efficiency of water-powered systems. Evidence of the type of water wheels used at individual mills can be found by observing the layout of the buildings relative to the watercourse. The earliest mills often had a large wheel positioned centrally within the building, with a vertical shaft taking the drive to the upper floors, where it drove machinery by means of horizontal line shafts using a system of gears. In smaller structures, water wheels were often positioned outside the mill, though sometimes housed in a small outbuilding.

ROTARY POWER

As well as changes to the arrangement of water wheels themselves (see p. 10), experiments were made with different systems for driving machinery from the rotary power of the wheel. John Lombe's silk mill at Derby, built in 1721, transmitted power from the water wheels along horizontal shafts linked by toothed gearing to a vertical shaft; and this in turn drove the large circular throwing machines, which extended through the ground and first floors, and the ranks of small winding machines on the floors above. Subsequent systems, such as that at Arkwright's mill in Cromford of 1771, all used variations on line shafts and belts driven by wooden drums.

STEAM POWER IN MILLS

The problem with using water as the primary source of power was that seasonal fluctuations caused variations in supply levels. With ever-larger mills demanding ever greater power, and with great strides being made in the use of steam, it was not long before steam engines were being put to work in textile manufacture. In 1782 James Watt produced a steam engine that produced rotary power and could therefore drive machinery directly, and in 1786 an engine of this type was installed at Papplewick Mill in Nottinghamshire.

ELECTRICAL POWER IN MILLS

By the end of the 19th century the huge textile mills of Lancashire and Yorkshire were demanding vast power resources, and this led to the development of the specialist 'Lancashire mill engine' capable of producing up to 4,000 horsepower. At around the same time the first electric dynamos were introduced, allowing greater flexibility (see p. 24), and these in turn were driven by the great mill steam engines and, later, by steam turbines. The first cotton mill to have its machinery electrically powered by steam turbine was the Falcon Mill in Bolton, completed in 1908.

Industrial Machinery

WATER FRAMES

What kind of machinery was used in the evolving textile mills? If it was the spinning jenny and the flying shuttle (p. 69) which first moved spinning and weaving out of the home, it was the invention of the 'water frame' by Richard Arkwright in 1771 that paved the way for textile production on a truly industrial scale. Deriving its name from the fact that it was powered by a water wheel, this machine was able to draw out the yarn in a single motion between sets of rollers running at different speeds, which then wound it on to a rotating spindle.

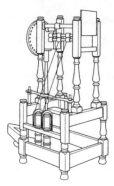

Water Frame

THE SPINNING MULE

A further improvement, known as the 'spinning mule' in reference to the fact that it was a hybrid between the spinning jenny and the water frame, led to even greater efficiency. At the same time, the weaving process was being increasingly mechanised, with the first power looms appearing by 1785 and improved versions, such as those installed at Quarry Bank Mill in Styal, Cheshire, putting the last of the old, skilled hand weavers out of business in the 1830s.

The design of the first generation of water-powered cotton mills was almost entirely determined by the need to position dual ranks of water frames and associated machinery. This led to an almost uniform arrangement of three or four storeys on a plan of about 72 by 30 feet (22m x 9m). Extra capacity was achieved simply by adding more storeys. The suggestion has even been made that some flagship mills, such as Stanley Mill, near Stroud in Gloucestershire, were designed specifically so that the machinery could be walked around and admired by the increasing number of 'industrial tourists' who visited such establishments from all over the world.

Developments in Design

STONE AND BRICK MILLS

The basic structure of Arkwright's mill at Cromford, built in 1771, set the pattern for the next 100 years. Load-bearing walls made of stone, or very occasionally brick, carried wooden beams on which the joists of the various floors rested. The windows in the first generation of stone mills were generally rectangular, while brick structures used segmental arches. Ornamentation was rarely applied, usually confined to the occasional pediment or window with classical styling. As a general rule, the age of construction can be identified by the size of windows, with those of the earlier examples, such as Calver Mill in Derbyshire, being smaller.

IRON-FRAMED MILLS

The problem faced by large, wooden-framed buildings was that textile machinery produced flammable cotton dust which presented a constant risk of fire. It was the need to reduce this risk that led to the introduction of iron-framed construction, an early example of which was Strutt's calico mill at Derby, built in 1792 using floors supported on narrow brick arches and cast-iron columns. As an extra precaution against fire, the underside of all exposed timberwork was coated with plaster. The world's first entirely iron-framed building is believed to be the Ditherington flax mill near Shrewsbury. Over time, load-bearing exterior walls gradually gave way to iron-frame construction with curtain wall cladding. A particularly elaborate iron frame can be seen at Stanley Mill in Gloucestershire.

INTRODUCTION OF CONCRETE AND STEEL

The larger machinery introduced towards the end of the 19th century led to a demand for larger spaces with fewer intermediate supports. This was met by the use of fabricated wrought-iron beams and later by rolled steel beams supporting floors made of concrete, an example of which can be seen at Centenary Mill, Preston, built in 1895. Since the load being taken by the exterior walls was now reduced, windows were made bigger – some of the larger mills of the last generation give the appearance of being constructed entirely with glass. At the same time, use was made of the latest industrially produced materials, such as the shiny red Accrington brick which is such a striking feature of surviving Lancashire cotton mills constructed up to the 1920s.

Lighting and Heating, Sanitation and Safety

▣ The first generation of textile mills needed to work long hours in order to repay the investment made in them. Since the need for load-bearing walls placed a limitation on the size of windows, this meant artificial lighting. But the huge number of candles that allowed Cromford Mill to operate through the night and impress visitors in the 1780s also represented a serious fire risk. So when coal gas using the Murdock system first became available (see p. 29) the illumination of the workplace was one of its earliest applications, such as at Salford Twist Mill in 1805. Within 10 years the firm of Boulton & Watt was supplying gas lighting systems to mills up and down the country.

At the same time, the efficient operation of textile mills depended to a large extent on the dexterity of their workers, and this in turn meant a requirement for adequate heating. The early mills were heated by open-hearth fires, but in the dust-filled atmosphere of the machine rooms these presented a serious hazard. One of the first solutions to the problem was the warm-air heating system developed by William Strutt at the North Mill in Belper, Derbyshire, and subsequently used in most of the mills in the county. The system was worked from a stove at ground level away from the main building, from which a flue rose through the building with outlet pipes on each floor immediately below ceiling level. Circulation of the warm air was assisted by small fireplaces located on each floor. An ingenious variation on the system was one used at Salford Twist Mill, built by George Augustus Lee in 1800, in which warm air circulated through the hollow cast-iron columns that formed the main structure of the building.

In case of fire, a means was required for quick escape from the building, and the better-designed of the early mills incorporated multi-access staircases housed within turrets on the external face of the structure. In some cases, such as the six-storey Calver Mill in Derbyshire, the octagonal turrets also included privies for the use of workers on each floor.

Ancillary Buildings: the North-lit Shed

One of the most enduring designs for industrial buildings emerged from the need to maximise natural lighting at the weaving stage of textile manufacture. From the 1820s, at mills in Lancashire, weaving sheds with north-facing windows and sloping roofs were being built, which, when built in numbers, formed a zigzag shape. One that was constructed at Manchester in 1829 had a capacity for 600 power looms. The so-called 'north-lit shed' was quickly adopted in other textile regions and, when adapted to more general uses, went on to become one of the most recognisable features of 20th-century industrial skylines.

Mill Building Façades

While it is true that the requirements for housing people and machinery led to a uniformity of basic design in textile mills, there could still be variation, and even such apparently functional buildings were often used to make statements on behalf of their owners. Even an unadorned massive, square, stone or brick building would be seen as a radical innovation in landscapes accustomed to smaller units of production, and could be seen to embody Enlightenment ideals of efficiency and rationalism that were prevalent at the start of the Industrial Revolution.

For reasons of economics, mill owners lavished the greatest attention to detail on what might be termed their 'flagship' buildings, those which through their large workforces and prodigious use of power could be used to symbolise the ambitions of their founder. The message that such buildings sent out was a threefold one. Primarily, the first generation of industrialists wished it to be known that they should be accorded an equal status with that rank of men who hitherto had held sway – the county gentry. Second, they wanted to demonstrate that manufacturing was not a temporary, somewhat vulgar adjunct to mainstream society but part of the very fabric of modern life. Third, they wished to embody in their landmark buildings the social ideals – such as uniformity, punctuality and sobriety – that they demanded of the newly massed ranks of labour.

PALLADIAN FAÇADES

The most ostentatious of the first generation of mills thus shared many of the architectural features of the Palladian country houses that were being built on the greater landed estates at the time. One of the most famous examples is Richard Arkwright's Masson Mill at Cromford, Derbyshire, built at the height of his fame and constructed in brick, with rusticated stone quoins. The

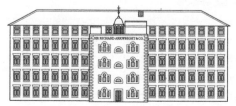

Facade of Masson Mill

central bays of its front elevation are lit by eight Venetian windows, and three in the Diocletian style, despite the fact that this part of the building accommodated only the main staircase and lavatories. However, to demonstrate that such lavish ornamentation was at this stage the exception rather than the rule, it has been estimated that only seven out of over 40 mills constructed in the Cheshire town of Macclesfield between 1780 and 1832 can be said to have been 'Palladian' in style.

POST-NAPOLEONIC FAÇADES

The move towards a more general application of architectural style to industrial buildings, and with it a greater sense of social order and stability, can probably be associated with the aftermath of the Luddite disturbances of the immediately post-Napoleonic era. Textile mills from this period throughout the country started to incorporate decorative features such as stone cornices, corners ornamented with pilasters and entrances highlighted with rusticated arches or stone pillars. An outstanding example is Stanley Mill in Gloucestershire. Although the building was constructed mainly of brick, the ground floor incorporated finely rusticated stone, and stone quoins were incorporated throughout. The central bays of the main elevation have Venetian windows and, in general, the building has been interpreted as the self-confident statement of the values of the emergent factory system, as well as heralding a new era in which the industrialist should be seen as being on equal terms with the county gentry.

ITALIANATE FAÇADES

While some mill buildings reflected little more than passing fashions in style, such as the extraordinary Temple Mills building in Leeds, completed in 1840 in an impressive Egyptianesque style, the general trend was towards the incorporation of more profound architectural values. In Yorkshire and Lancashire in the 1850s there was a discernible move towards an Italianate style, noticeable also in some of the newly built country houses of the area, but perhaps more significantly associating the mill's owners with landmark architecture such as that of Osborne House, Queen Victoria's new residence on the Isle of Wight. One of the first examples was Gilnow Mill, Bolton, which when completed in 1858 incorporated a six-storey Italianate tower, dentilled cornices, string courses and pairs of pilasters at the corners and at the most prominent parts of the façade.

The high point of this ostentation was undoubtedly Saltaire Mill, constructed by the entrepreneur and philanthropist Titus Salt in the 1850s on the banks of the River Aire near Bradford. The very size of the building – at 560 feet (170m) in length it was proudly declared at the time of its construction to be comparable with St Paul's Cathedral – declared its owner's ambition. In practical terms, it incorporated all the latest ironwork, both cast and wrought, in its magnificent roof structure and was designed to be fireproof throughout.

But it is in the sheer exuberance of the architecture that Titus Salt declared both his ambition and the place of manufacturing in society. The principal chimney was constructed to look like an Italian campanile, at 250 feet (76m) tall deliberately just higher than the famous Monument in the City of London. Throughout the building, doors, windows and other exterior detailing deliberately confuse the visitor into thinking that the building is a Renaissance palace. Titus Salt, and the other great mill owners of his generation, were to be seen as no less than the heirs of the great wool merchants of medieval Florence, as had been the Medici 400 years before them. It is not difficult to imagine the founder's self-satisfied pride when, at Saltaire Mill's opening in 1853, the Mayor of Bradford declared that their generation had built 'palaces of industry equal to the palaces of the Caesars'.

FACTORIES

From Mill to Factory

Industrialisation, then, brought with it radical changes in the nature of work. Since the greatest acceleration of change was in textile manufacture, for much of the period, in certain areas at least, that word 'mill' remained in use to describe the buildings in which the work took place. But as the system spread to other areas of manufacture, a word that was originally an abbreviation for 'cotton manufactories' came into common use. For most of the 19th and 20th centuries, therefore, any workplace employing large numbers of people in specialised tasks, for at least some of which a source of power was supplied, was known as a 'factory'.

THE FACTORY ACTS

In Britain the word came into more widespread use following the passing of a number of 'Factory Acts' from 1819 onwards. Throughout its history, the factory was a place where employees were required to perform routine tasks under supervision and within prescribed hours. In its earlier incarnation the factory system employed men, women and children, though originally with some demarcation of roles – men would be working the spinning mills, women doing 'lighter' work such as 'carding' (separating the cotton fibres), and children scrambling among the machinery as 'piecers' and 'scavengers', picking up scraps of loose cotton from the floor. For most of the 19th century, the majority of factory workers were first-generation newcomers to the area, usually from the surrounding countryside, though often from further afield such as the large numbers of Irish immigrants who settled in Lancashire in the aftermath of the Great Famine of 1845.

CHILD LABOUR

The first generation of factories was notable for the employment of large numbers of children, often brought long distances from urban workhouses and orphanages. Child labour was cheap, and useful for undertaking tasks requiring difficult access. Perhaps the greater incentive for employing children was, however, the desire to accustom workers to a harsh regime at an early age. That being said, at times of full employment factory work could be relatively well paid. Women and children generally outnumbered men in the workforce, and factories provided one of the few opportunities for women to earn a separate wage.

MASS PRODUCTION

A second significant phase in the development of the factory system came with the introduction of mass-production methods towards the end of the 19th century and, in the 20th, the evolution of the production line. By this time the factory was the primary force in shaping the way people lived and worked in Britain, and one that had a massive influence on settlement and transport patterns, transforming much of the landscape in its wake.

Developments in Factory Construction and Design

The traditional view has been that factories were conceived of as single large units from the start. However, it is equally plausible that they derived their plan from agricultural buildings in that the typical factory, up to the end of the 19th century at least, was not a single building but a group clustered around a courtyard. Surrounding the complex was an outer perimeter wall, which defined both the limit of ownership and the area within which the owner had effective control over his workers' lives. The main requirement was space for people and machines, and a reasonable level of natural lighting. Although a large number of the early mills had been built of stone, the second generation of factories were commonly built of brick, the cheapest and most readily available durable construction material until the arrival of reinforced concrete in the 1920s.

AUTOMATIC MACHINERY

In their essential design, factories developed along the same lines as the textile mills until the mid 19th century and the introduction of automatic machinery and machine tools. Automated production systems were adopted with particular rapidity in the United States, which suffered from a shortage of skilled manpower at the very moment of its main push towards industrialisation. As so often, processes initially developed for the manufacture of armaments quickly moved into other areas of production. It was not long also before the so-called 'American System' of mass production, by which industry was organised towards the production of large numbers of identical, relatively small components requiring little operating skill, moved across the Atlantic to Britain and Europe. During the 20th century, the most significant developments in the design of factories went hand in hand with ever-increasing automation and use of production lines.

DAYLIGHT ARCHITECTURE

The next significant phase of change in factory design occurred between the two world wars and is perhaps epitomised by the Wet Processes Building designed by Owen Williams for the Boots pharmaceuticals company at Nottingham between 1930 and 1933. Conceived according to the principles of 'daylight architecture', the factory was generously lit by floor-to-ceiling windows augmented by circular glass lights set into the concrete roof and allowing light to flood down through wells surrounded by galleries and linking bridges. Rising as it did to meet the manifesto of the modernist movement, the building was described by one contemporary critic as 'law and order in planning, construction and working'.

It was the introduction of electric power into the factory environment that brought about the most significant change in the 20th century. From this point onwards, instead of a situation where all machinery was run by belts and line shafts from a water wheel or steam engine, each machine could have its own appropriately sized power supply. This not only led to an opening up of space on the factory floor, it also meant that some of the ancillary buildings of the industrial environment, such as coal sheds, could be removed.

Factory Façades

REGIONALISED STYLE
Following the high point reached in the design of the mill exterior with buildings such as Saltaire Mill, industrial architecture became a legitimate subject of contemporary debate, especially with regard to style and choice of materials. Whether particular buildings were constructed according to Renaissance or Gothic principles was often influenced as much by regional as by national tastes, as can be seen in the broad trend towards Italianate themes in the textile factories of the West Riding compared with the Gothic prevalent in large parts of Lancashire. However, a common trend was towards the use of innovative, industrially derived construction materials such as glazed brick and faience tiles. Similarly, while civic buildings such as banks might be expected to be stone-built in a sober classical style, it was more readily acceptable for industrial buildings to make

quite ostentatious use of ceramics and ironwork within their Renaissance or Gothic façades.

The significance of regional variation can be seen in a city like Birmingham. Here, the diversity of the local industrial scene meant that there was no one dominant type of factory building, yet the city can be seen to have developed quite a distinctive architectural style. So whereas some of the landmark civic buildings were constructed to classical and Italianate designs, the industrial façades were predominantly Gothic, many of them the work of local architect J.G. Bland, responsible also for the stylistic uniformity that can be seen among the carpet factories of nearby Kidderminster.

ARCHITECTURAL EXPERIMENTATION

This trend for local experimentation, which started in the later 19th century, probably reached its peak in the 1920s in such buildings as the Wrigley's gum factory on the outskirts of London, built in 1926 to an idiosyncratic design incorporating elements derived from the recently discovered tomb of Egyptian boy-king Tutankhamun. While that particular example has recently been demolished, the Pyrene and Hoover factories on London's Great West Road survive as evidence of the jazzy modernist style employed by architects for many of the so-called 'bypass factories' of the period.

RETURN TO FUNCTIONAL DESIGN

The economic depression of the 1930s witnessed a return to more sober exterior designs incorporating plain brickwork and simple cubic masses, with any decorative effects being limited to a single central feature. At the same time, the 'Modern Movement' was elevating the status of the factory as a celebration of the vibrant creativity of the age and promoting the ideal of a purely functionalist architecture, the unique purpose of which was the accommodation of industrial processes. This particular trend was to have a lasting impact, first of all in the 'shadow factories' built during the Second World War, then through the industrial estates of the post-war period (see p. 93), to the windowless and featureless steel-clad monoliths constructed close to main transport hubs at the end of the industrial period in the 1990s.

WAREHOUSES AND WHARVES

The Industrial Revolution led to a huge increase in production of a great range of goods. At the same time, the need for raw materials such as cotton from the United States, and the increasing international trade that came with higher levels of economic activity, all prompted a need for renewed provision of warehouses, storage facilities and places of loading and unloading.

However, the great numbers of wharves and inland warehouses that proliferated during the period were not just places for storing goods awaiting sale. They were also places where goods could be kept while awaiting payment of duty, or where the manufacturer could display his wares; sometimes they even formed an integral part of the factory premises. Whatever their uses, many warehouses and transhipment facilities rank among the architectural gems of the Industrial Revolution. As with the mills and factories, those who built and used them knew that these great structures, which often dominated the centre of textile towns and harbour fronts, could be used to project a positive image of industry.

Quayside and Railway Warehouses

Among the first transhipment facilities to be constructed in the industrial period were the quayside structures in the North

East of England – known locally as 'staithes' – from which coal dug in the area was taken around the British coast by ship. The impetus to build these often quite complex structures came from a desire on the part of mine owners to keep coal stocks at the coast ready for shipment rather than at the pitheads. Coal was loaded into wagons which were taken by horse-drawn trams on wooden rails across country to the point where they were run down wagon ways on to drops by which the material was delivered into the holds of ships. In time, wooden rails were replaced with iron, and horses with steam locomotives (see below). With the later development of canal and railway networks, particularly in northern and midland England, the number of inland warehouse facilities proliferated.

TRANSHIPMENT POINTS

The first large-scale warehouses built to serve canals were probably those erected at Castle Fields in Manchester in the 1770s to serve the Bridgewater Canal. From this time onwards, transhipment points developed at various places on the canal network (see p. 92) and sometimes grew into independent communities in their own right – as such, perhaps the earliest specialised industrial communities in Britain. The best example is probably Stourport-on-Severn, built at the end of the 18th century at the point where the Staffordshire & Worcestershire Canal met the River Severn (see p. 100). Within a short time, Stourport effectively became an inland port between the Midlands and the sea. Here goods were transferred from canal narrowboats to larger river craft bound for Bristol and the South Wales ports. With its elegant brick warehouse complex, surmounted by a clock tower, Stourport reflects the aspirations of the early phase of the Industrial Revolution.

Similar facilities developed at Shardlow in Derbyshire, at the junction of the Trent & Mersey Canal and the River Trent.

Cheddleton Flint Mill, Staffordshire, which ground material for the pottery industry using the power of twin water wheels.

Pleasley Pit Head, Derbyshire, a rare survival from the golden age of British coal power.

*Battersea Power Station, London, Sir Giles Gilbert Scott's
'cathedral for the electrical age'.*

*Killingholme Oil Refinery, Lincolnshire, entered service in
1968 and processed 10 million tons of crude oil per year by
the early 21ˢᵗ century.*

Blists Hill Blast Furnaces, Shropshire; power houses of the industrial revolution behind a medieval gothic facade.

Levant Tin Mine Cornwall, with typical beam engine house dominating its coastal setting.

Quarry Bank Mill, Styal, Cheshire, symbol of the ordered elegance which its founder Samuel Greg sought to impose on the developing cotton industry.

Albert Dock, Liverpool; functional triumph and a high-point of Victorian industrial self-confidence.

Gas Street Basin, Birmingham, historic terminus of the profitable Worcester and Birmingham Canal.

St Pancras Station, London, a soaring gothic fantasy that has aroused stronger emotions than almost any building of the industrial age.

Glenfinnan Viaduct, Inverness, one of the last of the great railway engineering works and harbinger of a future world of concrete.

New Lanark, Lanarkshire, which soon became the largest industrial enterprise in Scotland and a model paternalistic community.

Saltaire, West Yorkshire, where the wealthy philanthropist Titus Salt founded a community that rewarded hard work and diligence and an industrial complex 'equal to the palaces of the Caesars'.

Recently-restored back-to-back houses in the former 'cotton capital' of Ancoats, Manchester. In the early 19th century they were breeding grounds for virulent diseases such as cholera.

Blackpool Seafront and Tower, Lancashire. The annual escape there by the greater proportion of the workforce of the North of England helped to make life in the industrial towns and factories at least tolerable.

Entrance to Egyptian Avenue, Highgate Cemetery, London, one of a number of urban ventures set up on a commercial footing to deal with an unavoidable consequence of burgeoning populations in the industrial cities.

Warehouses on a more spectacular scale were built at Ellesmere Port, where the Ellesmere & Chester Canal reached the River Mersey. Built originally in 1795, the town continued to grow until the 1850s, at which point it went into temporary decline in the face of competition from the railways. However, Ellesmere Port witnessed a revival in its fortunes following the completion of the Manchester Ship Canal in the 1890s.

INLAND WAREHOUSES

By the 1830s railways had taken the place of canals as the primary means of transport of goods and materials, and the warehouses built at this time on the Liverpool Road in Manchester by the Liverpool & Manchester Railway Company epitomise the growth in scale that the shift helped to create. Brick-built in three storeys and 20 bays with a basement, the warehouses were a striking addition to the industrial landscape of the area. Soon, railway goods depots were being built all over the developing network, providing interchanges between rail and both the canal network and the improving road system. A good example is the depot that was built in North London where the London & North Western Railway and Great Northern Railway lines crossed the Regent's Canal.

The high point of Victorian railway warehouse architecture was undoubtedly the GNR warehouse built in Manchester in 1896. This featured a multi-level rail, road and canal interchange with effectively two goods stations, one on top of the other. The enormous five-storey building took in goods at the connecting point of the Bridgewater Canal and the new Manchester Ship Canal. Its massive, relatively plain exterior was enlivened by the use of red and blue brick, with giant lettering advertising the pre-eminence of the proprietor company. Recently renovated, the warehouse also has the distinction of being one of the first large steel-framed buildings in Britain.

Manufacturing Warehouses

⌗ One of Britain's oldest industrial concerns, the Coalbrookdale Company, was one of the first to invest in ornate warehousing with which to advertise its products. The first of these, a large building of 1838 with iron window frames and sills, was later adorned with a decorative iron clock tower, all of which served to demonstrate the company's skills. In 1840 it constructed a castellated Gothic building on the bank of the River Severn a little way upstream from the famous iron bridge, a conspicuous advertisement of the company's continued presence in the birthplace of industrialisation itself. From the 1850s, buildings such as this were able to show off the latest technology in the form of gas lighting and steam heating.

The great Yorkshire textile mills typically had warehouses set at a right-angle to the main range. The most impressive surviving structure is probably that built at Manningham Mill, Bradford, between 1871 and 1873. This was a vast building of 44 bays, constructed with iron columns and beams supporting concrete arches, all designed to render the structure fireproof. Larger windows provided ample light for workers to sort the raw wool at one end of the building, and for owners and prospective buyers to examine finished cloth at the other. The entire façade was adorned with Renaissance detailing that matched the exuberance of the boiler chimney, designed to resemble an Italianate campanile.

WAREHOUSE QUARTERS

During the mid 19th century distinctive warehouse quarters developed in most of the textile towns, one of the most famous being in the part of Bradford known as Little Germany. Here, the typical complex had large gateways giving access to internal yards, sometimes covered to keep goods hidden from the view of competitors. On the ground floor were hydraulic presses used for packing, and other steam-powered machinery used in rolling, folding and measuring cloth. Greatest attention, however, was given to the finely detailed doorways through which potential customers would enter into halls lit by gas before making their way up ornate staircases to view the wares on display on the floor above.

A similar concentration of impressive structures was to be found in Nottingham's Lace Market, which included the premises that the Adams & Page company built in 1854–5 to an 'E' shaped plan mimicking the style of an Elizabethan country house. The building was of five storeys and included rooms for machining and packaging lace, large open areas for displaying products, and even a library and projecting chapel to complete the illusion of landed as opposed to industrial wealth.

The high point in design of the textile warehouse was reached in Manchester in the 1890s, when enlarged facilities were required to meet the soaring output of the Lancashire mills. The greatest concentration of buildings was on Whitworth Street, where a number of vast steel-framed buildings included offices as well as warehouses. The arrangement of windows was designed to maximise internal light levels, and large archways allowed motor vehicles to drive straight through the main working halls, where goods were loaded and unloaded with movable cranes. Although the buildings were designed for maximum functionality, the self-confidence of their owners was demonstrated in the dramatic French baroque styling, which incorporated decorated granite and terracotta façades.

Fort Dunlop

A final flourish of this generation of ornate storage facility came with the Dunlop Rubber Company's Fort Dunlop warehouse of 1925, built on the outskirts of Birmingham and itself modelled on the dramatic Lancashire textile mills of the interwar period. Constructed of brick, steel and concrete with a glazed loading canopy, the building was of 44 bays with large windows, and still provides a dramatic backdrop to entries into Birmingham by train from the north.

Warehouses for International Trade

The growth of international trade through British ports during the 19th century prompted the development of major new facilities at docks in London, Liverpool, Bristol, Hull, Glasgow and Manchester. Traditional quayside facilities had been relatively small, rarely more than four storeys high, and with timber beams and floors that presented a significant fire risk. The second generation of warehousing at major ports were constructed on an altogether grander scale and, in a move towards fireproofing, incorporated all the new industrial materials.

The first major project was St Katherine's Dock, next to the Tower of London, on which work commenced in 1825 under the joint supervision of engineers Thomas Telford and Philip Hardwick. In their designs the two men aimed for maximum quayside length and storage space, and for facilities that would as far as possible avoid the necessity of double handling. This was to be achieved primarily by means of overhead cranes that took goods straight from ships' holds to the appropriate floor of the warehouse. The result was an impressive group of six-storey warehouses, square, compact and functional but with a ground-floor arcade of massive cast-iron Doric columns combining rugged functionality with a crisp uncluttered classicism. While the construction methods employed in the original buildings were fairly traditional, a central block added in the 1850s incorporated an iron frame and stone-flagged floors. Despite suffering extensive bomb damage during the Blitz, St Katherine's Dock was able to remain in operation until 1968. In the 1970s work began on converting the site to a modern complex including marina, apartments and offices.

One of the most impressive of Liverpool's industrial heritage sites, Albert Dock, was a logical progression from St Katherine's when work began in the 1840s. It too included an open-plan arcaded ground level for the handling of goods, once again to a design of elliptical arches supported by cast-iron Doric columns, which provided support for a number of internal hoists as well as space for cranes. Railway lines on either side of the buildings ran to dockside transit sheds. A good deal of engineering innovation was incorporated into the design, including iron columns, tension rods and roof trusses, and the brick façades were built almost flush with the granite dock walls, virtually eliminating uneconomic double handling of goods. In terms of detailing, the cast-iron Tuscan portico and classical ornamentation mark a high point of Victorian commercial self-confidence, and, once derided, Albert Dock is now viewed as a supreme monument to the Industrial Revolution.

INDUSTRIAL ESTATES

The final phase of factory and warehouse design came with the development of the industrial estate in the late 19th and early 20th centuries. The concept of industrial zoning, whereby manufacturing and warehousing facilities were separated from residential areas, developed initially from pioneering developments of the late 19th century. The first of these was established by the Scottish Co-operative Wholesale Society at Shieldhall, on the outskirts of Glasgow, and the second, the

Trafford Park estate at Manchester, which was commenced in 1896, went on to become one of the most important industrial sites in Britain.

Ebenezer Howard and Industrial Zoning

If any one individual is to be associated with the concept of industrial zoning it is Ebenezer Howard whose books, including *Garden Cities of Tomorrow*, provided the theoretical basis that underpinned what was probably the most significant movement in architecture and planning of the 20th century. As a direct result of Howard's ideas, a number of estates were laid out in the South of England including Letchworth (1903), Slough (1918), Welwyn Garden City (1919), and the immediate post-war foundations of Harlow, Crawley and Milton Keynes.

Of particular importance was the government endorsement of the concept, particularly as a means of relieving unemployment, which resulted directly in the establishment of sites at Team Valley in County Durham, Treforest in South Wales and North Hillingdon on the outskirts of Glasgow. After the Second World War, industrial zoning was a major plank in the edifice of governmental planning policy, often centred on redundant military bases and sites formerly used by heavy industry.

Trafford Park shared the same designer as the Manchester Ship Canal, which it was largely constructed to serve. By the early 20th century, ocean-going ships had direct access to the great metropolis of the Lancashire cotton industry, and the massive new industrial estate was designed to capitalise on this further. The most important development at Trafford Park was the establishment of the Ford motor factory in 1911, which was the first major transfer of American mass-production technology to Britain, though American expertise had already led to the construction of a huge engineering works by George Westinghouse in 1901. At its peak during the Second World War, when products manufactured at Trafford Park included the famous Lancaster bomber, 35,000 workers were employed on site, most of them commuting from various parts of the Greater Manchester area by electric tram.

CHAPTER FOUR

TRANSPORT

Just as industrialisation was concerned with moving people to places of work, it was also dependent on moving raw materials and fuel to factories and finished goods to warehouses and markets. As a result, the Industrial Revolution witnessed a parallel 'transport revolution' as entrepreneurs, seeking cheapness in everything, strove for ever greater efficiency in the movement of large numbers of people and things.

For centuries, transport in Britain had relied on rivers and roads. While river transport was largely a matter of keeping waterways free of obstruction, between the end of the Roman period and the later 18th century few significant improvements had been made to the country's road network. The revolution in road building that occurred at this time was due largely to the pioneering work of three men – John 'Blind Jack' Metcalf (1718–1810), John Loudon Macadam (1756–1836) and Thomas Telford (1757–1834). Metcalf's main contribution was to appreciate the need for firm, well-drained foundations, while

Macadam and Telford went on to develop new techniques in road surfacing using small broken stones. By the 1820s these new methods had been widely adopted, and for the first time in 2,000 years the main limitation to the speed of road travel across much of Britain was the physiology of the horse rather than the condition of the road.

However, while road improvements made a great difference to the ability of people to get around – particularly through the development of the stagecoach network – when it came to the bulk movement of materials and goods many practical difficulties remained. Heavy loads meant slow journeys, by horse and cart or long-distance packhorse trains. Those with money tied up in mines, warehouses and factories could ill afford inefficiency and delays, and the first major focus of their capital investment was the improvement of the inland waterway system, particularly through the construction of canals.

Canal construction provided an impetus to industrial growth on a scale that could hardly have been envisaged, and it led in turn to the development of new mechanical means of transportation. The first of these was the railway, the supreme culmination of decades of improvement in the harnessing of steam to provide power. By the end of the 19th century the transport revolution this brought in its wake had transformed Britain physically, socially and economically. During the 20th century the development of motor transport meant that the people of Britain could take once more to the roads *en masse*. No sooner had they done so than they took to the skies, and by the end of the industrial age the relationship between people and the world they inhabit had changed forever.

CANALS

The significance of canals as the first means of inland movement of bulk commodities cannot be overestimated. Compared to the Continent, Britain was in fact quite slow to adopt a canal system, but once work started the network developed quickly. Much of the impetus was provided by the desire to move coal more economically, and it was this that first brought about the fruitful partnership of Francis Egerton, Earl of Bridgewater (1736–1803), and the engineer James Brindley (1716–72) that was of such significance to the engineering of canals in Britain.

Development of the Canal Network

The first canals in Britain were small-scale affairs constructed as a means of supplementing the existing river navigation system. Then, from the middle of the 18th century, some local schemes were developed as a means of opening up the coalfields of the Midlands and North West of England. The first of these was the Sankey Brook Navigation that joined the St Helens coalfield to the River Mersey, opening in 1757. Its immediate success attracted the attention of the Earl of Bridgewater, who operated profitable coal-mines at Worsley, 5 miles (8km) to the west of Manchester. Constructed by John Gilbert and James Brindley and completed in 1761, the Worsley to Manchester canal effectively halved the price of coal in the Manchester market. As a result, industrialists started investing heavily in canals, and the transport revolution had begun.

The Earl of Bridgewater made sure that he and his chief engineer remained at the centre of affairs, and the next significant development was a link between the Worsley to Manchester canal and the River Mersey at Runcorn, by which time the whole waterway was known as the Bridgewater Canal. Next came the Trent & Mersey, or 'Grand Trunk Canal', which made the first connection between the Midlands and Lancashire and took its route through the Staffordshire Potteries at the prompting of Josiah Wedgwood, one of the scheme's promoters. In the same year, 1766, work had started on the Staffordshire & Worcestershire Canal, which proceeded southwards from a junction with the Trent & Mersey to join the River Severn at Stourport in Worcestershire. Two years later, the link from this scheme to Birmingham, known as the Birmingham Canal, was the start of a complex canal network around the Midlands centred on Birmingham, which was instrumental in the economic development of the heavily industrialised region that became known as the Black Country.

The high dividends paid by the first of the canal schemes led investors to look further afield. In 1790 the Forth & Clyde Canal opened, greatly facilitating the economic development of lowland Scotland between Edinburgh and Glasgow. In England, the canal builders who had met with such success in forging links between the rivers Mersey, Trent and Severn turned their attention to connections with the Thames and the lucrative London market. This was first achieved by the opening of the Thames & Severn Canal in 1792 and subsequently by the Kennet & Avon Canal, which took a more southerly route through Bath and Devizes to Newbury, opening in 1810.

Most of the 19th-century canals were larger and more heavily engineered than their predecessors. They included the Grand Union Canal, which joined the Midlands system at Rugby and Leicester to the Regent's Canal in London, at the terminus of which the Limehouse docks were completed in 1820. Once these major routes had been completed, engineers set about adding the remaining links in the chain, starting with the Leeds & Liverpool Canal, which made the connection between the two great industrial hubs of Yorkshire and Lancashire. Soon afterwards the Shropshire Union Canal was completed to serve the coalfields and ironworks of one of the earliest industrialised parts of Britain, and then the Newport, Monmouth and Brecon canal system which transported coal from the Monmouthshire valleys to the sea. The latter, as well as providing a boost to the iron and coal industries of South Wales, stimulated the growth of urban centres at the coastal ports, such as Cardiff and Newport.

The great vision of the 19th-century canal builders was to link the English Channel with the Bristol Channel, in effect connecting the two great commercial centres of London and Bristol. However, though a number of sections of the projected Grand Western Canal came into use, the full scheme was never realised. Short systems were also constructed in the North East of England to take coal to the ports, and one of the last substantial engineering feats undertaken by Thomas Telford, the Caledonian Canal along the Great Glen in Scotland, was completed in 1822 but was never of great commercial importance.

In 1750 there had been about 1,000 miles (1,600km) of river navigation available in Britain; 100 years later, as a result of canal building, 4,250 miles (6,840km) of inland navigation were in existence. However, even the great engineering improvements of the Victorian era could not shield the canals from the competition presented by the railways from the 1830s onwards. By 1850 much of the canal system was being bought out by the railway companies and allowed to run down, though there were occasional agreements reached with the canal companies enabling sections of the two systems to serve each other. After the middle of the 19th century, therefore, the story of Britain's canals was one of decline and abandonment until the realisation, in the mid 20th century, that parts of the system could profitably be reopened to service the leisure market.

Gauges

Canal Lock

🔲 One of the difficulties faced by the canal system was that it was not uniform throughout the country. Most of the first generation of canals built in the Midlands and North West of England were fairly wide, with a gauge of about 14 feet (4.27m), which helped where canals connected with tidal water systems. Those inland routes built in undulating terrain, and where water supplies were restricted, were generally constructed on a narrow, 7-foot (2.13m) gauge. Finally, in areas where gradients were particularly steep, tub boat canals with an average gauge of 6 feet 4 inches (1.9m) were used.

The standard for the narrow-gauge waterways was set by the Staffordshire & Worcester and Trent & Mersey Canals, both the work of James Brindley and completed in 1772 and 1777 respectively. It was a pattern soon followed by much of the system that encircled Birmingham and also that of South Wales, both of which involved large numbers of locks and tunnels (see p. 103) and therefore needed to minimise as far as possible on engineering costs. Tub boat canals were built quite extensively in Shropshire and the South West of England.

Even within these three general groupings there were numerous minor variations, and the lack of uniformity meant that the canal network was never able to become a single integrated system. In general, narrowboats were able to travel anywhere south of a line between the rivers Trent and Mersey, and the wider craft anywhere to the north. The barges used on the main navigable river systems, such as the Trent, tended to be larger still. The varied topography of the British Isles meant that much of the canal system was heavily locked and encountered problems of water supply at summit levels. For much of Britain, in particular large parts of Scotland and the South West of England, artificial waterways were never an economically viable proposition.

Getting across Country

LOCKS

Canal engineers in Britain had to come to terms with crossing large areas that were not flat. The main method used for climbing hills was the lock, which consisted of an enclosure built of brick or stone, generally rectangular, and being of the minimum dimensions capable of handling the largest craft on that part of the system. In this way, minimum use of water was achieved. In the Midlands, therefore, a typical 'narrow' lock had a chamber about 7 feet (2.13m) wide and some 76 feet (23m) long, which allowed for some extra length for the inward-opening gates at of the lower end.

A boat proceeding downhill required a full lock, and once it was inside the chamber the gates would be closed and sluices at the low end would be opened to allow water out. Once the level inside the lock was the same as the lower, downstream level, the gates were opened and the boat could pass through. For boats travelling uphill the procedure was the reverse. Where water needed to be pumped into locks, steam engines of the beam type were commonly used.

Where great differences of level occurred in a relatively short distance, groups or 'flights' of locks were often used. The biggest in Britain is at Tardebigge on the Worcester & Birmingham Canal, where a flight of 30 narrow locks took boats to an elevation of 217 feet (66m) over about 2 miles (3.2km). At Devizes a flight of 29 wide locks takes the Kennet & Avon Canal out of the Vale of Pewsey. This system is particularly spectacular since the locks are very close together and in an almost completely straight line. A variation on these arrangements was the 'staircase' in which the top gate of the lower lock forms the bottom gate of the one above. A good example is at Foxton, where the Leicester branch of the Grand Union Canal descends an incline by means of two staircases of five locks each.

INCLINED PLANES AND LIFTS

The problem with long flights of locks is that, apart from encountering difficulties with water supply, they could cause significant delays to traffic. From the 1780s, therefore, canal engineers started to look at other ways of solving the problems presented by steep changes in gradient. One of the most common was the inclined plane, by which boats were lowered down a slope by a winch system. Although there is no longer one in use, these can still occasionally be identified in the landscape. An example is that at Ridd on the Torrington Canal in North Devon.

One of the best preserved – and most spectacular – is the Hay Inclined Plane, which was put into operation at Coalport in Ironbridge Gorge, Shropshire, in 1788. The challenge here was to take boats carrying coal from Blists Hill to a canal running parallel to the River Severn 207 feet (63m) below. It was solved by a system whereby tub boats full of coal were floated on to a cradle, hauled over a bank and then wound mechanically down

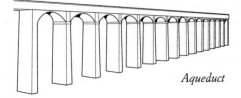

Aqueduct

rail lines to the lower canal, where the load was transferred to canal boats. The empty boats were then hauled up again, by 1793 with the aid of a steam engine.

The only canal lift that has remained in use in Britain is at Anderton, near Northwich in Cheshire, a feat of engineering widely considered to be among the greatest of the 19th century. The mechanism was constructed in the 1870s to connect the River Weaver Navigation and the Trent & Mersey Canal, which at this point came to within about 400 feet (120m) of each other, with a vertical distance of about 50 feet (15m). It consisted of a large gantry carrying an aqueduct from the canal basin above, from which a lift system lowered boats to the river below. Originally powered hydraulically, the lift was converted to steam power by the 1890s, and in 1908 to electricity.

AQUEDUCTS, TUNNELS AND CUTTINGS

While locks were the main system used to take canals up and down hills, the canal builders also used tunnels and cuttings for going through them, and the principal means for crossing valleys was the aqueduct.

From the first time they were employed as an engineering solution, aqueducts caught the imagination of industrialists and public alike. One of the pioneer structures was Brindley's Barton Aqueduct on the Bridgewater Canal, constructed in 1761. It was described by one contemporary as a 'castle in the air' and remained in use until it was replaced by the equally dramatic swinging aqueduct of 1893. More typical of Brindley's work was the Dove Aqueduct on the Trent & Mersey Canal near Burton-on-Trent, which is 1¼ miles (2km) long and consists of 23 low brick arches. The pinnacle of Victorian canal engineering came with the use of cast iron in aqueduct construction, a supreme example being Telford's construction at Pont Cysyllte near Llangollen in North Wales, which opened in 1805.

The early canals were built as cheaply as possible. Brindley's Staffordshire & Worcestershire avoided prohibitive engineering outlay by following the contours of the land, resulting in a long circuitous route. This did not present too great a problem at a time when there was little competition from alternative routes and boatmen's wages were low. However, on many stretches of canal there was no alternative to a tunnel such as those constructed on Brindley's Trent & Mersey Canal at Preston Brook, Saltersford, Barnton and Harecastle. In an effort to keep costs down, early tunnels like the original one at Harecastle, in Staffordshire, had a relatively small diameter, or 'bore'. This meant that boats had to be 'legged' through, the boatmen lying on narrow boards projecting from the side of the boat and walking along the sides of the tunnel to push the boat along.

The greater engineering efficiency of later canal routes came about as a result of increasing competition from roads and railways and resulted in the building of longer tunnels such as the second one at Harecastle, completed by Thomas Telford in 1827. The longest canal tunnel in Britain is the 3.1-mile (5km) Standedge Tunnel on the Huddersfield narrow canal, opened in 1811. The very last canals to be constructed were made as straight as possible, which necessitated an even greater amount of engineering. For example, Telford's Birmingham & Liverpool Junction, completed in 1835, had long stretches of earthworks including the 2-mile (3.2km) long Tyrley cutting, the deepest in the country.

Ports and Quays

⌨ Such was the commercial significance of many of the transhipment points along the canal network that they resulted in concentrations of facilities which in some cases developed into independent communities (see p. 88). At the smaller end of the scale were canal-side wharves that never became more than villages but would still include paved surfaces for facilitating access of goods, a small warehouse, a lime kiln, weighbridge and crane. A good example is Fradley, in Staffordshire, home to a small community of canal workers that grew up around the pub at an isolated junction.

On the large scale were the ports and quays that developed into towns with a proliferation of buildings including warehouses, stables for boat horses, boatyards (where boats were built and maintained), workshops to service the passing trade and, of course, cottages and a pub for resident boatmen and visitors alike. Runcorn, where the Bridgewater and Trent & Mersey Canals joined the Mersey, is a good example of the larger community. Here, basins and quays were constructed at the top of the flight of 10 locks which descended to the river. Warehouses and cottages were built and the fledgling community was overlooked by the elegant three-storey Bridgewater House from which the Earl supervised much of the early work.

At Stourport-on-Severn, basins were constructed for the transfer of goods between the narrowboats of the canal system and the large barges that worked the River Severn. Around these were numerous large warehouses and stables, which were also a feature of the basin constructed at Shardlow at the junction of the Grand Trunk Canal, the River Trent and the main road from London to Manchester.

RAILWAYS

The large-scale engineering involved in canal building from the second half of the 18th century would have been the first real indication to people in Britain of the changes that were coming about with industrialisation. But it was the 'Railway Revolution' of the 1840s that made it abundantly clear that life in Britain had changed forever. As well as being a barometer of change, no other form of industrial technology took such a hold on the imagination of the people as the railways. At the same time, no other aspect of the Industrial Revolution had such a profound, and lasting, impact on the face of Britain itself, its landscape. This was evident not only in the massive engineering work that tied up a substantial proportion of the country's human and material resources, but also in the towns that were created by the railway companies. All told, there was hardly a community in Britain that was not affected – either directly or indirectly – by the coming of the railways.

The height of the railway boom – that heady decade between 1840 and 1850 – brought with it an expansion of all aspects of the national economy. Indeed, the railway industry itself became a major cog in the growing economic machine, as prices of the main industrial materials – such as iron, coal and bricks – started to move in tandem with the completion of railway contracts. In technological terms, the railways became the breeding ground for a whole generation of engineers, architects and entrepreneurs. By 1850 railway locomotives were burning coal at the rate of a million tons a year, and much of the expansion of the iron industry in the 1850s and 1860s was a direct result of demand from the railways. If there was one difference between the railways and the canals that had come before them it was that this remarkable new technology was a bulk mover of people as well as goods.

By the middle of the 19th century, the railway had well and truly entered the national consciousness, and the opening of new lines was frequently a cause for celebration and festivities. In terms of the development of the modern world, it was the first form of transport with which the mass of the population had regular contact, and there is no more eloquent demonstration of its hold on the collective psyche than the wave of nostalgia that greeted the demise of the steam locomotive at the end of the 1960s. The remarkable persistence of this phenomenon is evidenced by the continuing interest in railway heritage and steam preservation societies.

There was, of course, a downside to railway mania: the impact on other forms of transport was devastating. As we have seen, by the middle of the 19th century the canals were in almost terminal decline. On the roads, the long-distance mail coach, which had been the mainstay of transport in Britain for a generation, became virtually obsolete, and up and down the country the turnpike trusts which had flourished at the start of the century were wound up. In much of Britain there was a discernible deterioration in the condition of roads, the maintenance of which once again fell to the responsibility of overburdened local communities.

The Development of a New Technology

◫ The name most closely associated with the birth of the railway is that of the Cornishman Richard Trevithick (1771–1833). Trevithick was the son of a Cornish mine manager, and his experience with pumping engines led him to conduct experiments in applications of high-pressure steam from an early age. In 1801 at Redruth he built the first steam-driven road carriage to carry passengers. However, it was apparent from the general condition of the country's roads that the future of free-moving steam vehicles would be limited. Instead, Trevithick turned his attention to the construction of a locomotive that would run on rails.

Horse-drawn tramways, originally using wooden rails, had by this time become a common feature of the industrial scene, particularly in the coal industry where they were widely used as the most effective means of haulage over distance (see p. 17). At a time when landowners were increasing the rents payable by mine operators, the reduced friction provided by rails meant that heavy loads could be transported quickly and cheaply. Such systems were operated most efficiently in the North East of England and South Wales, where loaded trains took advantage of down gradients on the run from mine to port. Particularly in tourist areas some tramways were also used to carry passengers, and it is worth bearing in mind that railways had already started to prove their viability before the introduction of steam locomotion.

Trevithick first brought together the twin technologies of the railway and steam power with the successful construction of a steam locomotive at the Coalbrookdale ironworks in 1802, followed by another at a coal-mine at Merthyr Tydfil in South Wales. The relative success of these early ventures into railway engineering was built on by John Blenkinsop, who in 1812 developed a rack-and-pinion railway to take coal from the mines at Middleton to markets in the centre of Leeds.

Within 25 years of Trevithick's pioneering work, the steam locomotive was to prove beyond question its viability as the most effective means of long-distance transport. The Rainhill Trials of 1829 have gone down in history as one of the defining moments in the creation of the modern industrial world. Competing engineers had been brought to this Lancashire village to decide on the best method of hauling trains along the new Liverpool & Manchester Railway, then in the course of construction. Here it was that the engineer George Stephenson proved that with the efficient new boilers incorporated in his locomotive *Rocket*

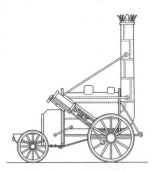

Stephenson's Rocket

moving steam engines were equal to the high demands of long-distance haulage. Of even greater significance among Stephenson's innovations was the direct drive from pistons to wheels that was the essential basis of all locomotive designs that followed – up to this point, all steam locomotives had essentially been beam engines on wheels.

The Development of the Railway Network

The first concentrations of railways were in the North East of England, where they developed directly from the early wooden tramways taking coal to the coast, and the Midlands and South of England, where they served the already complex canal system. Most of these early systems developed for the transport of coal. The success of the rack-and-pinion railway between Middleton and Leeds – claimed to be the first railway in the world and one that effectively halved the market price of coal in the area – was followed by the Stockton & Darlington Railway on which George Stephenson pioneered some of his early designs. Significantly, the Stockton & Darlington railway adopted the track gauge that had been established by the local colliery companies, and which became standard across the network. The one exception was the Great Western Railway, on which Brunel used a broader gauge in the interests of speed, efficiency and greater comfort. However, the inconvenience of having to change engines and rolling stock at the intersection with the other lines, plus the need for more land in broad-gauge schemes, meant that the GWR reluctantly converted to standard gauge, a process that was completed in 1892.

However, it was the Liverpool & Manchester Railway, which opened a scheduled service for both passengers and goods in 1830, that really set the railway age in motion. Despite the fact that all the earliest railways had been constructed with the needs of industry firmly in mind, patterns in traffic turned out to be quite different from what was anticipated. Records of carriage receipts for the 1830s show that, in fact, revenues from passengers were twice those from the transport of goods. Once it was obvious that large profits were there for the taking, the railway boom gathered pace and by 1836 nearly 2,000 miles (3,200km) of track had been completed, including most of the main routes in and out of London.

The first of these was the London & Birmingham Railway, a lasting monument to the engineering skills of George Stephenson, soon to be followed by routes out of the capital to Bristol, Southampton and Brighton, then lines to Lancashire, Yorkshire, the North East of England and Edinburgh. By June 1841 another great railway engineer, Isambard Kingdom Brunel, had left his lasting mark in the landscape in the form of the Great Western Railway from London to Bristol, and plans were underway for an extension across the River Tamar and into Cornwall. By the time of the opening of the Great Northern line between London and York in 1852, the national rail network as we know it was virtually complete. All the major industrial areas, cities and ports in the country were linked, and by the early 20th century, at which time a number of extensions were made to the coastal holiday resorts, Britain had the densest rail network in the world after Belgium.

Getting across Country

TUNNELS AND CUTTINGS
The large number of tunnels through which the railways of Britain pass is a reflection of the requirement for relatively level and direct routes through undulating country. It is also a reflection of the fact that much of the country's rail network was completed at a time when the technology of railway locomotives

was still at an early stage. The relatively low level of traction attained by the earlier engines meant that steep gradients had to be kept to a minimum. At the same time, owing to high land values, even in towns there was a proliferation of tunnels, bridges and viaducts. Paradoxically, fewer tunnels were constructed in the highland areas of Scotland and Wales, simply because there was less economic incentive for direct routes, so most took circuitous courses along valley bottoms. This also reflects the fact that much of the network in Wales and Scotland, such as the Glenfinnan Viaduct (see p. 64), was constructed relatively late, when the levels of investment available at the height of the railway craze were something of a distant memory.

The greatest number of tunnels can therefore be found in the Pennines, where the railway engineers worked to connect the great centres of industry, and in lowland England, where they often cut through hills that hardly seem to present much of a barrier at all. For example, the greatest engineering work undertaken on the London & Birmingham Railway was the Kilsby Tunnel in Northamptonshire, completed in 1837. Its course of almost 1½ miles (2.4km) is marked on the surface by a number of brick-topped ventilation shafts. Had the line been constructed 20 years later, the tunnel would probably not even have been considered. The Woodhead Tunnel through the Pennines between Sheffield and Manchester had, however, been unavoidable when it was constructed in 1845. The human cost of much of the great railway engineering works of the age is highlighted by the number of men who died there, either as a direct result of the building work on the tunnel or from disease in the crowded shanty towns where they lived on desolate moorland during the seven years of toil required to bring the work to completion. Hard facts such as this are all too easily forgotten in our admiration for these great works of engineering that are also great works of architecture.

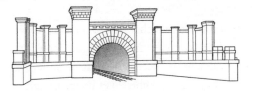

*Primrose Hill
Tunnel Entrance*

It was at tunnel entrances that railway architects let their imaginations loose in ways that could most freely celebrate this bold new arrival in the British landscape. One of the earliest examples of this exuberance was at the Primrose Hill Tunnel on the London & Birmingham line, where a dramatic Italianate façade made a fitting welcome not only to the capital but to the accession of the young Queen Victoria in 1837. Four years later, the 1¾-mile (2.8km) long Box Hill Tunnel on Brunel's Great Western Railway included a triumphal arch in a finely detailed classical style, which not only celebrated a remarkable feat of engineering but also advertised the new railway to travellers on the adjacent Bath Road. When railway engineers approached the Earl of Lichfield for permission to tunnel under his estate at Shugborough, in Staffordshire, he conceded on condition that the construction was of appropriate distinction. The architects duly obliged with a castellated entrance at one end and a work of fantasy-Egyptiana at the other.

Modern travellers on the Birmingham to London line take much of the engineering work through which they pass for granted. However, even some of the cuttings are in fact monumental achievements. That at Tring in Hertfordshire was cut in the late 1830s and is 2½ miles (4km) long and 60 feet (18m) deep. It is a sobering thought that all this work was accomplished by men using picks, shovels and wheelbarrows. Not only was the task laborious, it was also dangerous, and the men who undertook it, drawn from all corners of Britain, deserve to be remembered as much as Robert Stephenson, the line's chief engineer.

The varied topography through which much of the new railway system of Britain would pass meant that there are probably a larger number of bridges and viaducts per route mile than anywhere else in the world. A remarkable 24,000 such structures were added to the British landscape between 1830 and 1860 alone. The majority survive, many in use and, more remarkably still, many still demonstrating most of their original features. An impressive early example was the Victoria Bridge across the River Wear at Sunderland, built in 1838 with a span of 161 feet (49m). Just ten years later, the 181-foot (55m) Ballochmyle Viaduct was built by the Glasgow & South Western Railway on the line between Kilmarnock and Dumfries. It had the largest span of any masonry structure to be built in Britain.

It was not long before the latest industrial materials were being employed in the building of bridges and viaducts. In 1850 Robert Stephenson completed the Britannia Bridge across the Menai Strait between mainland Wales and Anglesey. Not only was this, at 1,500 feet (460m), the largest wrought-iron span in the world at the time, but it was constructed to a revolutionary new design incorporating tubular iron girders that Stephenson had used for the first time at nearby Conwy in 1847. The final memorial of the other supreme engineer of the period, Isambard Kingdom Brunel (1806–59), came with his Royal Albert Bridge at Saltash, which crossed one of the major barriers to the expansion of the railway network, the River Tamar between Devon and Cornwall. Faced with the formidable problem of bridging tidal water at a height of 100 feet (30m) – required to give adequate clearance to shipping – Brunel responded with a bold design incorporating elliptical iron tubes and a 300-ton iron cylinder providing support mid-water. By the time the bridge was opened amid great ceremony by Prince Albert in 1859, Brunel was ill, but he managed to make his own first crossing, on a couch placed on a flat truck, some days later. That autumn he died at the age of 53 and Britain mourned the premature passing of one of its greatest servants, memorialised on his final achievement with the inscription 'I.K. Brunel – Engineer – 1859'.

A final, heroic phase of construction came with the bridging of the remaining obstacles to the railway network in the form of the Rivers Tay, Forth and Severn. The first of these, the original bridge across the Tay built in 1878, ruthlessly exposed the over-ambitious engineering that was the downside of self-confidence when it was swept away the following year during a violent storm as a train passed over, with the loss of 75 lives. Its successor was an improved version of the wrought-iron lattice girder construction, the last of the great wrought-iron bridges, and at 10,711 feet (3,265m) it is still the largest railway bridge in Britain. Three years later, in 1890, came the grand finale of Victorian bridge building in the extraordinary shape of the Forth Rail Bridge, revolutionary not only in its radical canti-lever design but in its use of mild steel instead of wrought iron. Such is the scale of this truly monumental structure that its maintenance is used as a byword for a never-ending task. It is, beyond doubt, one of the most spectacular monuments to the industrial age.

By the end of the 19th century steel had become the primary material for large-scale construction works in Britain. At the same time came the first use of the material that, together with steel, was to change the face of Britain in the 20th century – concrete. One of the last railway viaducts to be built in Britain was the magnificent example at Glenfinnan on the Mallaig extension of the West Highland Railway, built using the new material and completed in 1898.

Railway Stations and Termini

⊡ While tunnels were the first railway structures to be given lavish architectural treatment, once lines were completed it was to their termini that architects turned their attention. Tunnels could usually only be seen for a fleeting moment and even then could only impress passengers already on a train. A station, on the other hand, was there for all to see, often near the centre of a town or city. More than anything it advertised this newfangled way of travelling – if potential passengers were not drawn to the station, how likely were they to get on the train?

An interesting observation concerning the great railway termini of the Victorian age is that no single style dominated, even at a particular time. Neither were architects and designers primarily influenced by the existing surroundings. On the contrary, almost all of the great stations appear to have been built to make bold statements reflecting the aspirations of the railway companies and the engineers they employed. If there is a single discernible theme it is that, more often than not, railway stations were designed to look like something else; to invoke comforting feelings of a familiar past, one based on paternalism and order. The technology might be radical and new but – despite some highly publicised accidents – people need have no fear of it.

The first of the great stations were those designed by Philip Hardwick for either end of the line when the London & Birmingham Railway was fully opened in 1838. Both were built in a neoclassical idiom – Curzon Street, Birmingham, with its Ionic columns and façade, and Euston, including a Doric arch. As such they echoed the stately homes of the preceding generation, with the obvious intention of suggesting that Britain's first intercity passenger line could be regarded as reliable and its owning company as a respectable concern. If those passengers taking the first journeys felt they were taking something of a leap into the unknown, at least at the point of departure and arrival they would be on familiar ground.

When Isambard Kingdom Brunel set to work on the design for the western terminus of his own great railway enterprise he looked to a past that, as well as carrying an air of authority, was specifically nationalistic. With its impressive mock-Tudor façade, Temple Meads station had an immediate impact on the Bristol urban landscape, one which, as the most complete early railway station in the world, can still be enjoyed today. The style was imitated at Carlisle Citadel station when it opened in 1847, though in the same year the architect J.P. Pritchett returned to the neoclassical idiom at Huddersfield. With a Corinthian portico six columns wide and two deep, the building dominates St George's Square in the centre of the town and was justly described by Sir John Betjeman as the most splendid railway station in the whole of Britain.

When Francis Thompson designed Chester station, opened in 1848, he was one of the first architects to employ an Italianate style that was to become popular in domestic and industrial architecture alike, a deliberate association of railway engineering with the supreme achievements of the Renaissance past. In the same year, however, H.A. Hunt returned to a more familiar English style at Stoke-on-Trent, where the station could superficially be mistaken for an authentic Jacobean manor house. Its benign paternalism was copied in other buildings in the town and was used again, on a smaller scale, at other stations on the North Staffordshire Railway, thus becoming something of a recognisable 'house style'.

It was the desire for corporate recognition that informed the decision of the Midland Railway Company to choose a bold design when it finally gained a foothold in the capital at St Pancras in the late 1860s. Both main components of its station fronting the Euston Road are on a massive scale, completely dwarfing its earlier neighbour of King's Cross. The railway shed was designed by W.H. Barlow and incorporates a huge wrought-iron roof with a span of 240 feet (73m), the work of the famous Butterley Iron Company. But the hotel building that fronted it, designed by George Gilbert Scott and opened in 1876, was even more impressive. A soaring Gothic fantasy complete with high roofs, spires and a majestic clock tower, it has aroused stronger emotions than almost any other building of the industrial age. It is again largely due to the efforts of Sir John Betjeman, a man able to see the poetry within the Victorian railway system, that the restored buildings can be enjoyed in all their glory today.

SHIPPING

By the middle of the 19th century Britain was becoming known as 'the workshop of the world' – not without reason, since a little under a half of the world's output of manufactured goods originated in British mills, factories and workshops. At the same time, over a quarter of the entire volume of international trade passed through British ports. Probably at no other time has one country had such a prominent position within the world economy.

Increasingly sophisticated facilities developed at coastal ports to handle this huge volume of trade, and by the early 20th century these had absorbed a level of investment equal to that of the canal system, which had itself heralded the Industrial Revolution. Following the success of the railways, the industrial period was also one where people's horizons opened up to a world of undreamed-of possibilities for travel. At the height of 'railway mania' Brunel had himself dreamed of fully integrating the railway network with the ports so that a single ticket could, for example, take a passenger from anywhere in Britain through Paddington Station in London to New York.

Ships and Shipbuilding

🔲 The early centre for manufacture of iron-hulled steamships was the Thames below the Port of London. It was there in 1836 that Brunel started work on the *Great Western* paddle steamer, launched the following year, that of Queen Victoria's coronation. Its successful maiden voyage to New York proved that a steamship could cross the Atlantic without running out of coal, a proposition that Brunel had calculated mathematically. The new paddle steamer had the advantage of speed, reliability and comfort, though it had needed to resort to traditional sail in mid crossing since the paddles were not so effective in ocean swell.

However, the biggest drawback was that it was very expensive to build a wooden ship strong enough to take the stress from the engines. Yet at this time the size of iron ships was limited by the problem of iron's effect on magnetic compasses, a problem that was overcome by the development of the correcting magnet compass system. Not until hulls were built completely of iron could the potential of steam be fully realised in shipping, and even then Brunel became convinced that the screw propeller would be more efficient than paddle wheels. These twin developments were realised in the launch of the steamship *Great Britain* in 1843, which likewise made a successful maiden voyage

SS Great Britain

to New York and proved itself to be one of the supreme engineering achievements of the Victorian age.

By the 1840s Brunel was incorporating wrought-iron plate in his design for the huge steamship *Great Eastern*, intended for voyages to India. Work began in 1851 and culminated in the vessel's launch from the Isle of Dogs in 1858. Once again a successful transatlantic crossing was made, but the frantic schedule leading up to launch had laid too much strain on the ship's inventor. Brunel's health failed and he died of a stroke the following year.

In the second half of the 19th century, the main shipbuilding centres shifted away from the restrictions of an increasingly crowded Thames to the North East of England (Jarrow and Wallsend), the North West (Birkenhead), Scotland (Clydebank) and Northern Ireland (Belfast). In 1900 Britain was building more ships than any other country in the world, with 60 per cent of global tonnage being launched in its waters each year. However, the depression of the 1920s and 1930s hit this sector of heavy industry particularly hard and the main shipyards, such as those at Jarrow and Clydebank, suffered debilitating levels of unemployment. Given a boost by the armaments programme leading up to and during the Second World War, the country's world position declined in its aftermath, as Japan's in particular rose, and continuing problems regarding infrastructure and labour relations precipitated decline during the 1960s. There are relatively few remains of the great shipyards of the 19th and 20th centuries still to be seen, the most complete being at Birkenhead and Wallsend.

Ports and Docks

▨ Following improvements made to facilities on the River Clyde between 1773 and 1781 which enabled Glasgow to become one of the most important port cities in Britain, major engineering works were undertaken throughout the country. Between 1750 and 1830, some 370 acres (150ha) of wet docks were constructed in England alone. During the 19th century London managed to maintain its position as the country's major port, but Liverpool took over second place from Bristol, which in time was also overtaken by Hull, where new docks were completed in 1829, Glasgow and – following the construction of the great Ship Canal in the 1890s – Manchester. The rapid decline in the fortunes of Bristol has meant that the main core of its dockside facilities has been fossilised and provides one of the best opportunities to view a port of the earlier industrial period. With the coming of the railways, dock companies moved towards handling goods quickly using transit sheds with rail lines on either side, such as at the Poplar docks in London built in the 1860s.

Towards the end of the 19th century, the increasing size of ships threatened Liverpool's position as a passenger port, with much of its traffic being taken over by Southampton during the 1890s. The opening of the Manchester Ship Canal effectively created a new seaport at Manchester, and after a slow start it rose to the position of Britain's fourth busiest port by the start of the First World War. The early 20th century also saw the development of new facilities at Immingham and Hull on the Humber, and at London. Southampton's position was consolidated between the First and Second World Wars, when it became the principal port for transatlantic and colonial journeys.

With the advent of container shipping and much larger vessels, only deepwater facilities could remain economical into the second half of the 20th century. The famous docks at London and Liverpool both went into decline from the end of the 1960s, while at the same time Felixstowe on the Suffolk coast developed into the busiest container port in Britain. Although much redevelopment of historic British ports has taken place over the last few decades, especially in London, Liverpool and Manchester, there is still a good deal of the original layouts that can be discerned. Liverpool's waterfront, in particular, survives as a significant part of the country's industrial heritage.

MOTOR TRANSPORT

The personal freedom ushered in by the railway found its ultimate expression in the industrial period with the motor car. Once the technology of the internal combustion engine had been developed at the end of the 19th century it was quick to find large-scale application. Already by 1904 there were 8,000 private cars on Britain's roads, in addition to 5,000 motor buses and 4,000 goods vehicles. Ten years later, at the outbreak of the First World War, there were over 100,000 cars alone; within another two decades the figure was well over a million.

If the first great transport revolutions, in the form of the canals and railways, had a great impact on the landscape and culture of Britain, that of the motor car was massive. By the early 1960s there was already a perception that there were too many cars on the roads, and town centres, in particular, were suffering from intolerable levels of congestion. The government, however, reached the opposite conclusion, that there were simply not enough roads for the cars, and the second half of the 20th century witnessed a massive extension of Britain's transport infrastructure, the impact of which was even more pervasive than that of the railways. The final phase of industrial Britain saw people and goods moving about the country with an urgency that would have been difficult to imagine when those pioneers of the steam age looked to a future in which man and machine would come together in the name of progress.

The Road to the Future

▣ In 1900, at the start of the motor age, the towns and villages of Britain were connected by a network of stone-surfaced macadam roads (see p. 97). While these had generally served well in the era of horse and cart, their unbonded surfaces suffered from the rubber wheels of the motor cars which sped by in clouds of dust. From the late 19th century, therefore, attempts were made to improve on existing road-building techniques, initially by surface spraying of tar. As the volume of motor traffic increased it became apparent that this was only a temporary solution, and in the early years of the 20th century county survey-ors started bonding road surfaces using the new 'tarred macadam' process. This was, however, an expensive and time-consuming business, and the greatest effort was naturally applied to consolidating major routes and to improving the quality of roads in urban areas.

In London, in particular, road improvement schemes in the 1920s and 1930s went hand in hand with 'slum clearance', the process by which the cheek-by-jowl cohabitation of people and industry was replaced by 'industrial zoning'. Away from the capi-tal there were major road schemes linking the main industrial conurbations of Manchester, Liverpool, Birmingham, Glasgow and Leeds. From an early stage, however, it was apparent that road building was a potential cause of controversy. The East Lancashire Road, work on which commenced in the early 1930s, was intended from the start as part of a two-lane network that would link the principal towns of this long-established industrial region. In the event, however, its progress was held back by disputes between rival local authorities so that several of the roads radiating from Manchester stopped abruptly at the bound-aries of councils which refused to co-operate with the city corporation.

Despite the much-heralded extension of personal freedom, in its early history the motor car was to many a rather brash and unwelcome intrusion. So, in an effort to keep people and cars at a healthy distance, urban planners of the inter-war period devised schemes to keep traffic away from town centres. Many of the bypass roads of the 1920s and 1930s, particularly around London, became the focus of industrial development themselves, such as the string of factories which sprang up along the course of the Great West Road constructed in 1925 in order to bypass Brentford. The best example of this phenomenon was the North Circular Road, which opened in the summer of 1934 to relieve congestion along the main routes into the capital. Within 20 years of its opening, the green fields which had lined much of its route had disappeared beneath the relentless spread of light-industrial and suburban development.

The second great phase of road building came after the end of the Second World War, when government was convinced that the development of a modern integrated economy required the swift and efficient movement of people, products and resources across the length and breadth of the country. The second half of the 20th century witnessed the construction of over 2,000 miles (3200km) of motorway, a process which commenced with the Preston section of what was to become the M6 in 1958, and the M1 to the immediate north of London in 1959. It would be no exaggeration to say that the motorways revolutionised the functioning of Industrial Britain, and by the mid 1960s the majority of movements of raw materials, finished products and all stages in between was being made by road haulage. By the end of the 20th century the direct heirs of the magnificent Gothic warehouses of Manchester were the massive, faceless, steel-framed distribution depots built at strategic points along the motorway network.

Bridges, Tunnels and Flyovers

🔲 The start of the 20th century saw a whole range of responses to the problem of how to distribute industrial development equally on both sides of major rivers. One of the most ingenious solutions to the problem of transporting both workers and resources across tidal rivers used by shipping was the transporter bridge. These were impressive structures constructed with steel girders on concrete bases. The high gantries allowed shipping to pass while people and vehicles were ferried across the river in a gondola suspended by cables and hauled across by a mechanical winch. Between 1905 and 1911 successful examples were installed across the River Usk at Newport, the Mersey at Runcorn and the Tees at Middlesbrough, all making a significant contribution to the establishment of heavy industry in their areas.

Similar large-scale use of ironwork was involved in the more conventional bridges constructed at this time. In a sign of the times, a number of these, such as the Queen Alexandra Bridge in Sunderland (1909) and the Trent crossing at Keadby (1916), incorporated both railway tracks and roads. One of the major public construction works of the inter-war period was the Mersey Tunnel, built for road traffic between 1925 and 1934. From the outset it was a thing of wonder with its electrical lighting and ventilation shafts with art deco styling.

A unique contribution to the history of bridges made by the development of the road network was the flyover, which allowed urban roads to cross other roads or canals. Significant structures of this type were built in concrete at Chiswick and Hammersmith in London in 1959 and 1961 respectively, soon followed by others in most of the major cities.

The Development of the Motor Industry

⊡ The first English-built motor cars to be produced in quantity are thought to be those that came from a converted cotton mill in Radford, Coventry, in 1897. At the opening of the works the year before, the Great Horseless Carriage Company, which operated the site in partnership with the Daimler Company, proclaimed it to be 'the largest auto car factory in the world'. Be that as it may, in 1900 the majority of cars on British roads were actually imported models from the United Sates and continental Europe. Once the motor craze caught on, however, manufacturing plants started to spring up in a number of towns and a British motor industry grew quite rapidly.

In many cases motor car manufacture developed from other industries, notably coach making and agricultural machinery. Oxford's long association with car manufacture came through the construction of bicycles, and in the metalworking towns of Birmingham and Coventry there was a somewhat unlikely transfer of technology and production techniques from the manufacture of sewing machines. At the other end of the scale, a significant number of motor engineers had first learned their trades in the big locomotive works.

Although the first purpose-built car factory, the works of the Dennis Company at Guildford in Surrey, opened as early as 1901, most early production was carried out on trestles in the standard manner of a typical machine works. The first moving assembly line was installed by the American Ford Motor Co. at its works on the huge Trafford Park industrial estate on the outskirts of Manchester in 1914. Other factories quickly followed, including the Arrol Johnston works built on a greenfield site on the edge of Dumfries in 1913, whose manager made improvements following a trip to the great car plants at Detroit.

Two companies that both installed modern assembly lines in 1926 – Morris at Cowley (Oxford) and Austin at Longbridge (Birmingham) – both went on to enjoy a long, if chequered, history of car production. Significantly, the Cowley plant had been given over to munitions production during the First World War, and for much of the 20th century there was a close relationship between the manufacture of armaments, motor vehicles and, as will be seen below, aircraft. Many of these trends are evidenced in the development of the Vauxhall Motor Co., which started out as a marine engine works established near London's Vauxhall Station in 1857. In the early 20th century the company started to manufacture motor cars and was taken over by the American General Motors Corporation in 1925. From that point its new factory at Luton grew rapidly, with a whole new wing being added during the Second World War for the production of tanks and other military vehicles.

In architectural terms, most of the smaller car factories from the early 1900s were based on a workshop system and reflected the building traditions of their locality. Since most were located out of view in the suburbs of cities such as Oxford and Birmingham, they were accorded little attention in terms of company advertising. Two notable exceptions are the office building of the Vauxhall Motor Co. in Luton, constructed in 1907 in a Queen Anne style and incorporating the company's wyvern brand-mark, and the Clement-Talbot works of the following year. Here the office building which faced the Barlby Road in North Kensington, London, was given the façade of a lesser country house, despite the fact that its core structure was actually an early use of reinforced concrete. With its covered drive-through entrance and cladding of Portland stone, it created an unquestionable impression of honesty and reliability to potential customers coming to inspect the shining new vehicles within.

Ford Cortina

The great motor plants of the 1920s and 30s were, however, on an entirely different scale. Ford's works on the Thames estuary at Dagenham, which opened in 1931, was modelled on its sister plant at River Rouge, Detroit, and similarly intended to be self-sufficient in resources. Iron ore was smelted on site and even the by-products of the coke ovens that supplied the blast furnaces produced the first tank of petrol for vehicles leaving the factory. The Dagenham works even had its own power station and reached the height of its fame with the production of the popular Cortina between the 1960s and 1980s.

Such was the scale of the motor industry by the inter-war period that it had the ability to transform the fortunes of entire cities. Attracting workers from all over Britain, the fastest growing city of this period was Coventry, the population of which almost doubled between 1919 and 1939. There were around 30 companies producing motor vehicles in the city's suburbs at this time, including Alvis, SS Jaguar and Triumph, and Coventry remained one of the primary centres of production until the end of the 20th century.

AIR TRANSPORT

In the final phase of the transport revolution the people of the industrial world, and the goods they made and imported, took to the air. Even more than the motor car, which enjoyed a great boost in production between 1914 and 1918, the aeroplane was a product born out of the requirements of mechanised warfare. Like the car, too, the manufacture of aeroplanes and aero-engines bene-fited from mass production techniques and assembly lines, and it is no accident that the firms involved in the leap in output which occurred in the 1930s and 40s were in the main car companies. However, unlike the car, in Britain at least, it was only in wartime that aircraft were produced on a truly mass scale. From 1937 much of the car plant at Cowley, for example, was turned over to manufacture of military aircraft and the famous Merlin engines – themselves the product of another car manu-facturer, Rolls-Royce – that powered iconic aircraft such as the Spitfire and Lancaster.

But it was not just the manufacturing side of the air transport industry that was transformed by war. During and immediately after the Second World War most of the old grass runways of British airfields were given hard concrete surfaces. Just as much as improvements in design and technology, this simple fact provided the boost that made air travel a commonplace experi-ence by the end of the 20th century.

Aircraft Production

⬚ As was the case with early motor car manufacture, the pioneers of aircraft design and construction were often engineers who had learned their trade in the locomotive industry. They included men like A.V. Roe, who established his first works under a railway arch in Hackney in 1908, moving production two years later to a redundant mill in the heart of Lancashire cotton production in Ancoats, Manchester. The requirement for large numbers of aircraft during the First World War prompted the construction of large factories and implementation of mass-production techniques from the start at works such as the iconically named National Aircraft Factory No. 1 at Waddon, in Surrey.

It was in the area around London that the early centre of the industry developed. However, the requirement for larger aircraft, and for greater numbers, during the rearmament programme of the 1930s and during the Second World War meant that much production relocated to the traditional heartland of British industry in Lancashire. These included the various factories in the Manchester area established by A.V. Roe to serve his Avro company which manufactured, among other aircraft, the famous Lancaster bomber.

One of the systems developed by wartime planners was that of the 'shadow factory', whereby the output of one aero-engine plant, for example, would be 'shadowed' by another as a precaution against air-raid damage. In that they were built to a standard form taking its basic design from the zig-zag north-lit roofs of the old weaver's sheds, they were to leave a legacy in factory construction that lasted to the end of the 20th century. Furthermore the fact that they were often established in areas of high unemployment, such as the West Midlands, had an impact on the industrial geography of Britain beyond the wartime period.

Air Travel

⊡ Britain's first official airport was established near the site of National Aircraft Factory No. 1 at Croydon by Imperial Airways in 1920. Terminal buildings and a hotel were added between 1926 and 1928 and the site became the focus of international air travel during the 1920s and 30s. However, much of the infrastructure constructed for air travel in the interwar period was based on the assumption that it would be in direct competition with the domestic intercity services provided by the railway companies. Indeed, some routes were established by the railway companies themselves, such as that between Cardiff and Exeter, where the rail equivalent was circuitous and required changes.

Thirty-five municipal airports were licensed by the authorities between 1929 and 1937, and obtaining such a licence was seen as a matter of civic pride by successful applicants. These included Blackpool, Cardiff, Ipswich and Wolverhampton, and some ventures, such as the joint Leeds-Bradford airport at Yeadon, established in 1931, continued to operate into the 21st century. Some airport sites that were less successful in the longer term, such as Derby and Sunderland, had a new lease of life at the end of the industrial period when they were converted to manufacturing sites for Japanese motor companies in the 1990s.

One of the most commercially successful airports in the world had its origins as an airfield known as Heath Row, established by aircraft manufacturer Richard Fairey in 1929. In 1944 the site was purchased by the government as a transport base for use in the war against Japan. In the event, that war was brought to a conclusion by atomic bombs dropped on Hiroshima and Nagasaki in August 1945, before the first runway had been finished. Instead, starting with a building programme initiated in 1947, the site was developed as a commercial airport later known as London Heathrow. By the end of the 20th century the airport was handling over 50 million passengers annually and was the third busiest airport in the world. As such, the world's first industrial nation remained at the centre of its transport networks to the end of the industrial period and beyond.

CHAPTER FIVE

READING INDUSTRIAL COMMUNITIES

The most enduring legacy of industrialisation was that it changed radically the way people in Britain lived, both in terms of their material conditions and in how they interacted with one another. Early industrialists had to work hard at attracting a workforce to factories that were often away from established centres of population, and at keeping them there. This trend, set in areas such as the valleys of the Pennines and the upper Clyde, was followed in the colliery villages and model communities of the late 19th and early 20th centuries. It continued in the centrally planned garden cities of the inter-war period of the 20th century, creations influenced by social theories of industrial and residential zoning and general social improvement.

Behind many of the developments over the roughly 200 years of the industrial period lay the notion that the new concentrated populations of working people that were being created could and should be kept in check, governed, controlled and improved. Yet many of what we now see as 'typical' industrial towns with a predominant manufacturing element developed more organically – as what might be termed 'open' as opposed to the 'closed' communities established by individual industrialists – and here the factory owners had to find other means of social control.

There is no doubt that the most profound impact of industrialisation was social as much as economic. It was the establishment of a substantial new gradation within society of men, women and children whose lives were directly tied to the production of raw materials in mines and quarries, and of finished goods in mills and factories. By the middle of the 19th century this group had become known as 'the working class', and the composite culture, outlook and aspirations of its members were to have a dramatic and lasting influence on British society throughout the industrial period and beyond.

CLOSED COMMUNITIES

Factory Villages

⊠ One of the first problems that Richard Arkwright had to overcome when he founded his first mill at Cromford in 1771 was the lack of a labour pool of suitable size. Although some of his workforce was drawn from among the local farmers and lead miners, most came from further afield in response to an advertisement placed in the local newspaper. By bringing workers in from outside the immediate locality he was committed to providing them with housing and social facilities. After all, Cromford at the time was little more than a hamlet, but as effective landlord, local squire and mill owner Arkwright assumed a degree of social control of his workforce, which would have fitted in with his plans. In time cottages, shops, a school, chapel and market were built at Cromford, which became, in effect, the first factory village.

The difficulties faced by Arkwright in finding labour were shared by most of the owners of the new textile mills, located as they were near vital supplies of water power and away from large centres of population. It was this that precipitated the use of children taken from workhouses and orphanages and accommodated in 'apprentice houses' such as those that survive at another Derbyshire mill, Cressbrook. Conditions for children both in the houses and in the mill, where they worked long hours doing dangerous jobs (see p. 83), were harsh. Discipline was seen as the key to efficiency in production, and there are features of mills, such as the bells that survive on many of their roofs, that speak of a highly regulated existence. This, more than anything, was the main difference from the working conditions of previous generations. Mill owners did at least increasingly include an element of education in the children's days, but this was usually fitted in at the end of a long day's work.

At New Lanark, which by 1793 comprised a complex of four mills, making it the largest industrial site in Scotland, the philanthropic industrialist Robert Owen saw workers' housing as the most vital link in the chain of production. In addition to providing decent living conditions Owen established a wholesale shop on-site where families could obtain basic provisions without eating too much into their wages. This was effectively the start of the co-operative movement, which was to play an important role in the improvement of conditions for the working class, especially in the 20th century.

Similar principles were put into practice by Samuel Greg at his state-of-the-art mill at Quarry Bank, near Styal in Cheshire. The first building, commenced in 1783, was already massive, consisting of 18 bays and five storeys. Over the entrance was a clock and, on top of the roof, a bell mounted within a cupola, both symbols of the order which Greg required of his workers. By the 1840s Quarry Bank was one of the largest mill complexes in the North West of England, whose buildings exuded a simple elegance and whose landscaped grounds were part of Greg's designs for encouraging a contented workforce.

The culmination of the textile phase of the factory village was Saltaire, the complex of mill and model community founded by Titus Salt in 1851 with the aim of creating 'a population of well-paid, contented, happy operatives'. The living accommodation was allocated in a deliberate hierarchy of architectural types, the intention being to instil the notion that hard work and diligence would pay off in the form of social improvement. As well as the houses themselves, workers at Saltaire were provided with communal dining-rooms, an educational institute and Congregational church. If the latter two suggest that Salt's primary aim was social control, by the 1870s he had shown that he had his workers' interests firmly at heart through the provision of a hospital, bath-houses and a school.

Transport Towns

A prime indicator of the economic and social impact of the transport revolution that went hand in hand with industrialisation was the emergence of communities that, from an early stage, became focused on key points in the transport network. At the same time, many of what we might call 'transport towns' clearly reflect their founders' aspirations in their architecture. On a significantly larger scale than the factory villages, the canal and railway communities were the first 'industrial towns' and, in both layout and architecture, were an important influence on the more varied communities that followed and on much of the urban landscape that is still with us today.

THE CANAL TOWN

Perhaps the best known and most rigorously planned community to develop on the canal system was Stourport-on-Severn, built towards the end of the 18th century at the intersection of the Staffordshire & Worcestershire Canal and the River Severn. The town, whose layout was influenced by the canal architect James Brindley, developed as a transshipment centre focused on the locks between the canal system and the river. It incorporated a port and dockyards, a new bridge and markets, a fine brick warehouse with clock tower, grand merchants' houses, workers' cottages and a large public house. Within a short time of its foundation 'industrial tourists' started to come from other parts of the country to marvel at this splendid new creation, and the town became a centre of the local social scene where fashionable ladies and gentlemen would attend regattas and other public events.

Shardlow in Derbyshire developed near the point at which the Grand Trunk Canal joined the River Trent and was also intersected by the main road from London to Manchester. Basins and warehouses were constructed for the movement of goods between canal-boats and riverboats, and workshops and boat-yards provided maintenance facilities. By the late 1780s, when the town was thriving, the wharves were lined with merchants' houses and gardens.

Ellesmere Port at the foot of the Wirral peninsula was created in the 1790s to give the Ellesmere Canal designed by William Jessop and Thomas Telford access to sea-going vessels via the Mersey estuary. By the early 19th century a number of houses and shops had grown up around the dock area. Expansion was rapid as workers moved to the new town, attracted by work at the docks and in associated industries. Unlike towns such as Stourport and Shardlow, which contracted once the main canal boom was over, Ellesmere Port had a second lease of life with the opening of the Manchester Ship Canal in 1894, followed by the establishment of nearby Stanlow oil refinery in the 1920s and numerous other industries in the course of the 20th century.

Goole, in the East Riding of Yorkshire at the junction of the River Ouse and the waterway known as the Dutch River, was developed from a small village of only 450 inhabitants in 1821 to a thriving market town with the opening of a new deep-water channel. As well as the usual facilities of wet docks and warehouses, in 1823 new streets and a market place were laid out. A deliberate attempt was made to give an appearance of elegance by alternating low terraced cottages with taller housing. The town developed rapidly as a result of the profitable coal shipment business and, in the second half of the 20th century, survived by adapting to the export of steel, timber imports from the Baltic and general container traffic.

THE RAILWAY TOWN

The best and most enduring examples of communities deliberately fostered by the railway companies are Swindon in Wiltshire and Crewe in Cheshire. Swindon was a small market town in 1810 when the construction of the Wiltshire & Berkshire Canal brought a boost in trade and, with it, population growth. In 1840 the area was chosen by Brunel and the Great Western Railway for a locomotive works, firstly because it was near the midpoint of the network, and also because it was the junction between the gentle gradient line to London and the more steep descent towards Bristol, meaning that trains would need to halt to change locomotives. In addition it was the point where the projected branch to Gloucester and Cheltenham would meet the main line.

Well-constructed terraces of houses were built for the company's employees around the entrance to the engineering works. In all there were about 300 two-storey cottages made of local stone to designs by Sir Matthew Digby Wyatt, who had also been responsible for Paddington station. Each house had a small garden at the front and a yard with wash-house and lavatory at the back. In addition there were shops and public houses. The streets, laid out in a grid pattern, were all named after towns along the Great Western line. A park was laid out on the edge of the new town. Social facilities at Swindon included a Mechanics' Institute, a church, a hospital and a lodging house for men working on the railways. Perhaps only Saltaire (see p. 136) provides a better example of industrial urban planning of this period.

Crewe, in Cheshire, was a similar development by first the Grand Junction Railway (from the late 1830s) and later the London & North Western Railway, again built around a locomotive works. From being a village with 70 residents in 1831, within 40 years Crewe had become a thriving town with a population of 40,000. In addition to the earlier housing the LNWR provided a doctor's surgery, gas and water works, public baths and a park.

Colliery Villages

The huge significance of the coal industry to the development of Industrial Britain is demonstrated most evidently by the surviving communities that developed alongside it. Despite the decimation of the industry towards the end of the 20th century a great number of these have survived. Although the term 'pit village' is common throughout the country, regional differences can be discerned among the communities that developed around coal.

Some of them were entirely new communities deliberately created around new deep pits sunk in the first quarter of the 20th century, especially in the North East, South Yorkshire and the area of the East Midlands known as 'The Dukeries'. At the start of the First World War only about 12 per cent of miners lived in company housing. The largest industrial communities of the 20th century were those built by the colliery companies, and their successor, the National Coal Board, was still providing houses for its workers in the 1950s.

COAL COMMUNITIES

Improvements in deep-mining techniques and a huge increase in demand for coal led to the growth of mining activity from the second half of the 19th century in the coal-fields of the Rhondda Valleys and South Wales generally, as well as in Scotland, the North East, the North West, Yorkshire and the Midlands. In many ways this mirrored earlier developments in the mills and factories, with large numbers of migrant workers needing to be brought in to fulfil capacity.

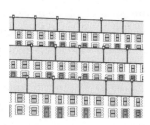

Rhondda Terraces

Up to the point where coal-mining was carried out on a truly industrial scale it had been viewed in many areas as a supplement to agricultural work, and traditional village life and mining existed side by side. But the new coal-mining areas were away from established centres of population, and new communities, complete with the necessary social facilities, needed to be constructed virtually from scratch.

Until the First World War most miners were living in communities that were already independently established. For example, mining areas in the Black Country and Shropshire, where operations were usually on a relatively small scale, were barely distinguishable from typical rural villages, with miners living in cottages next to workers in other industries, such as ironworkers. The new, larger mines, however, created separate closed communities. In South Wales, mining in Rhondda and the other valleys developed on a large scale from the 1840s as a result of the opening of the Taff Vale Railway and the expansion of Cardiff docks. By the 1890s there were no fewer than 75 collieries within the valley system. The relatively narrow valleys led to cramped living conditions, with lines of terraced houses strung out along the valley sides. Among the houses the prominence of Nonconformist chapels in Welsh pit villages provided a powerful symbol of their closed community ethos. Other social facilities reflected the dominant masculine culture that tended to develop in closed mining communities and included rugby football teams, brass bands and male voice choirs. In many cases the backdrop to the communities was huge spoil heaps, the inevitable result of the frenetic mining activity. At best these were an eyesore; at worst they were a real danger, such as the one at Aberfan, which collapsed in 1966, destroying 20 houses and a school and causing 144 fatalities, the majority being children. In the face of the decline in the industry it was a tragedy that, if anything, reinforced the spirit of a community whose very existence was under threat.

In contrast to the Welsh valleys, the pit villages that developed in the North East of England were generally quite compact. The Ashington Coal Company opened some of the country's most productive pits in Northumberland in the late 19th and early 20th centuries. Between 1898 and 1904 the company built around 850 houses, a number which had risen to 2,500 by 1914. Most of these were in new villages at some distance from established settlements, with the result that they fostered a keen sense of community. The earliest colliery houses in Ashington itself – which grew to be the largest pit village in the North East – were built in the local stone. However, the town was later dominated by a rectangular grid of brick-built terraces looking on to open green spaces, each terrace having small gardens and outside lavatories. Communal facilities, erected mainly in the 1890s, included chapels and co-operative stores. The development of the Northumberland coalfield continued between the wars, and in this region alone about 12,000 houses were built by the colliery companies, with support from central government, between 1922 and 1928.

The new mining settlements of the East Midlands coalfield known as 'The Dukeries' were set out by the mine owners of the early 20th century as 'model villages' intended to form stable communities for generations of miners. This area has some of the best-preserved communities of this type. A prime example is New Bolsover, in Derbyshire, where the village was planned as two concentric squares of solidly built brick and half-timbered houses facing a substantial central green. As well as the houses themselves – many of which were in a mock-Tudor style intended to evoke a past golden age – there was a school, shops, social clubs and public houses.

The other main area to be developed in the first quarter of the 20th century was the South Yorkshire coalfield. The pit villages in the vicinity of Doncaster were similarly influenced by the 'garden city' movement (see p. 94). An example is New Rossington, which was designed from 1916 as two concentric circles with green spaces in the middle and social facilities including schools, public houses and chapels. In contrast to the 'closed' communities of the Welsh valleys, the new model pit villages of South Yorkshire were provided with multi-denominational places of worship, which reflected the disparate nature of the communities that developed in the area, partly as a result of immigration from elsewhere.

From Model Village to Garden City

▨ Towards the end of the 19th century, despite a number of social reforms, it was evident that industrialisation brought in its wake the unwelcome side-effect of cramped, poor-quality housing and unsanitary living conditions. At the same time, industry itself was coming under attack for its alleged dehumanising effect on the men, women and children it employed; William Morris was not alone among social commentators when he railed against the 'tyranny' of 'bewildering factories'. The emergence of a number of philanthropically inclined industrialists at this time – men who wanted to celebrate the potential positive contributions of industrialism – was therefore of great significance. Whilst the previous generation had had its Titus Salt, this new era saw the rise to prominence of men such as Cadbury, Lever and Rowntree who wanted to test their assertion that entrepreneurial wealth generation need not be at the cost of the needs of the community. During the last century of industrialism, the 20th, their lead was in turn taken up by social theorists and central government planners in a well-intentioned attempt to engineer a brave new industrial world.

The first of these 'industrial reformers' was William Hesketh Lever, later Lord Leverhulme. In 1887 Lever started looking for a site on which he could expand his 'Sunlight' soap-making business, then based at Warrington. He settled on an extensive former marshland site in a prime location on the Wirral peninsula between the River Mersey and a railway line. The following year he set to work in his plan for a 'model community' in which he could house his workers at the factory site while at the same time attempting to restore 'that close family brotherhood that existed in the good old days of hand labour'.

Lever commissioned over 20 different architects and made each responsible for a different block of houses, so that styles varied from French Gothic to the Cheshire half-timbered vernacular. No expense was spared in building materials, which included Flemish brick imported from Belgium. By 1900, 400 houses had been built, and by the time the project was completed there were over a 1,000. In 1914 the village already had a population of 3,500. Each year a proportion of the company's profits was invested in the development of the village and its social facilities.

As well as constructing houses and allotments, Lever also promoted schemes for the welfare, education and recreation of his workers and encouraged the formation of local societies to promote participation in the arts, literature, science and music. By the time of its completion the village could boast a number of meeting halls, a cottage hospital, church, concert hall, schools and an open-air swimming pool. The centrepiece of the village was the Lady Lever Art Gallery, opened in 1922 in memory of the industrialist's wife, a symbol of the social ideals they had shared.

In 1879 the brothers George and Richard Cadbury decided to relocate their chocolate factory from premises in central Birmingham to a greenfield site about 4 miles (6km) to the south-west by the stream known as the Bourn Brook. As well as fitting in with their expansion plans, the site was explicitly chosen for its perceived benefits to the health and contentment of the company's workers. In 1893 they set about establishing a model village next to the factory to be called 'Bournville' which the family hoped would 'alleviate the evils of modern more cramped living conditions'.

By 1900 over 300 houses and cottages had been built, each with a garden, mostly in a 'traditional' style designed by the architect William Alexander Harvey and influenced by the contemporary Arts and Crafts movement. In keeping with their Quaker beliefs, the Cadburys tended towards restraint and hoped to inspire others to follow their example of a workers' community with the character of a rustic English village enhanced by the deliberate use of a restricted range of house-types in brick, tile and half-timbering. Quakers, like many others, saw drink as the 'scourge of the working man', and there were to be no public houses in the village. More generally the family were keen to promote the health and fitness of their workforce and provided facilities for a range of outdoor sports including a swimming lido.

The Cadburys' ideas were followed closely by Joseph Rowntree, their co-religionist and a fellow confectioner, in his own model village at New Earswick on the outskirts of York. He began work on it in 1900 with aspirations toward social improvement and providing solutions to 'the housing problem'. His houses were to be 'artistic in appearance, sanitary and thoroughly well-built, yet within the means of working men earning about 25 shillings a week'. As well as the cottages, again built mainly in the style of the Arts and Crafts movement, the village included a 'Folk Hall' (initially intended for the use of all religious denominations), a school and a doctor's surgery. Similar ideals were shared by the steel and shipbuilding magnate William Beardmore, who between 1914 and 1918 constructed a mixture of tenements and semi-detached villas adjacent to his main Glasgow works at Clydebank.

A particularly innovative example of private provision was Herbert Austin's workers' community at Longbridge, of 1916–17. Known as 'Austin Village' and built initially for his aircraft and munitions workers during the First World War, it comprised around 200 prefabricated American-style timber bungalows made of imported Canadian cedar. The village housed some 2,000 workers.

Many of the developments in planning and design of housing during the 20th century came about as a result of the 'garden city' movement originally inspired by the model villages created at Port Sunlight, Bournville and New Earswick. Of particular significance were the ideas of the social reformer Ebenezer Howard, spelled out most clearly in his book *Garden Cities of Tomorrow* (1902) in which he put forward his belief that manufacturing and residential housing should be kept apart in separate 'zones'. His ideals were a direct inspiration to the foundation of new zoned communities at Letchworth (commenced 1903) and Welwyn Garden City (commenced 1918) and were reflected in centrally planned settlements established under the New Towns Act of 1946 including Harlow, Crawley and Milton Keynes. Of these, Letchworth provides some of the best evidence for studying the development of the 'new town' phenomenon. In the centre was the main industry, the Spirella corset factory, cunningly disguised as a large country house. During the Second World War the factory was also used to make parachutes and decoding machinery for the war effort.

OPEN COMMUNITIES

Reading the Industrial Town

▣ Towns and cities based on more than a single industry – though in many cases there was one that was dominant – were the most typical communities built by industrialisation. Crowded, smoke-filled and unsanitary, they presented a massive challenge in terms of social cohesion, administration and public health. During the period of their rise, roughly from 1800 to 1870, they were characterised by a persistent failure in the quality of housing to keep pace with levels of immigration and social change. However, the end of the 19th century saw the development of philanthropic societies aimed at alleviating the worst problems, and the period after the First World War witnessed concerted efforts by local authorities to effect improvements. Indeed, the early 20th century is seen by many as something of a golden age for the administration of industrial cities in Britain. As well as being large-scale experiments in new ways of living (and dying), the industrial towns and cities saw the birth of new forms of recreation, education and entertainment that were to have a lasting impact on society and culture as a whole.

HOUSING

Until the advent of mass urban transport such as electric trams towards the end of the 19th century, most working-class families lived close to their place of work. In the industrial towns of the Midlands and the North of England one of the most common forms of urban housing was 'back-to-backs', twin rows of houses built in a 'terrace' sharing a rear wall in common. The first generation of back-to-backs was built in Leeds in the 1780s and 90s. Many of these remained in use, and this type of housing continued to be built well into the 20th century. In Leeds they were first put up by workers' building clubs, but it was not long before they became the most popular form of high-density housing among property speculators. Similarly common, especially in the densely populated industrial metropolis of Manchester, were multi-storey cellar dwellings in which the poorest inhabitants lived below ground level. More typical still were the hurriedly erected workers' tenements built around a central 'court', which was a particularly popular housing type in Sheffield.

In most towns, legislation of 1858 and local by-laws brought a gradual end to this type of housing by about 1900. Except in Leeds, Bradford and surrounding areas of West Yorkshire, the development of single-row terraces, often with tunnels giving into shared yards, was a distinctive feature in most industrial towns in England in the late 19th and early 20th centuries. Indeed, rows of these, even more than back-to-backs, are a characteristic image of the industrial town. Typically they comprised rented accommodation with two rooms and sometimes a small pantry or cellar. Census returns show that over 80 per cent of dwellings in England in 1911 were of terrace type. The length of terrace was only really restricted by topographical constraints.

Many very long ones were built in the mining valleys of South Wales, while one of the longest in the country was Silkstone Row in Lower Altofts, Yorkshire, with a length of about 800 feet (250m).

In most towns poor-quality, unsanitary workers' housing existed next to better-quality houses, but in the larger cities, of which London and Manchester are the prime examples, dense working-class 'slums' developed as speculators responded to the huge influx of migrant workers. In response, charitable housing organisations were formed such as the Metropolitan Association for Improving the Dwellings of the Industrious Classes, established in 1841. Much of their work was towards the replacement of back-to-back type housing with more substantial tenement blocks such as the block of flats built in St Pancras Road in 1847. One of the most famous organisations was the Peabody Trust, which was established in 1862 to help the poor of London and opened its first housing estate in Commercial Street in 1864.

In 1869 Liverpool became the first local authority to erect council houses on a large scale. The first slum clearances followed the passing of the Artisans and Labourers Dwellings Improvement Act of 1875, which granted compulsory powers to local authorities enabling them to buy up slum properties and either demolish or improve them. In a parallel development, during the 19th century there was a migration of middle-class residents from the old centres of towns towards the suburbs, which had developed in all the major cities by the 1840s. From this point onwards, a typical feature of industrial towns and cities throughout Britain was a distinction between 'west end' and 'east end', essentially one between residential suburbia and the dirty, overcrowded districts where large concentrations of urban poor lived alongside the factories in which they worked. The principal reason for this duality was that the prevailing westerly winds of the British Isles meant that those living to the west of industrial cities would be relatively free of the noisome smoke and smells that were pumped out in great quantity by the growing number of workshops and factories. Despite redevelopments that came in the wake of industrial decline in the 1980s, the distinction between east and west end can still be read clearly in the landscape of many cities. In Sheffield, for example, Sir John Betjeman identified the Broomhill suburb as one of the best preserved of the industrial era. Here the city's steel and cutlery barons built substantial stone houses in elevated leafy surroundings, limited yet still impressive copies of the mansions of the great industrialists such as Lord Armstrong's Cragside, at Rothbury in Northumberland, to whose splendid isolation they aspired.

WATER SUPPLIES AND SEWAGE TREATMENT

The rapid growth of towns during the industrial period presented considerable problems relating to the supply of water for both industrial and domestic consumption. From the end of the 18th century, to help deal with demand from rapidly increasing urban populations, small reservoirs began to be built by private companies. However, a royal commission of 1843–5 reported on the unsatisfactory and unhygienic nature of water supplies in the new industrial towns. The Public Health Act of 1848 allowed for local authorities to provide water supply, but some early schemes were over-ambitious and insufficiently engineered. Some notorious tragedies drew stark attention to the problem. On the night of 5 February 1852 the banks of the Bilberry reservoir at Holmfirth in Yorkshire

Derwent Dam

burst, leading to 81 deaths. More infamous still was the Sheffield Flood of 11 March 1864, which followed the bursting of the new dam at Dale Dyke reservoir and resulted in 240 deaths and the destruction of large numbers of buildings.

From the late 19th century a number of large-scale works were undertaken with heavily engineered banks and dams, and these included some of the greatest engineering feats of the industrial age. A good example is provided by Howden and Derwent dams in the Derbyshire Peak District on the outskirts of Sheffield. Here, the massive project, carried out between 1902 and 1916, included the quarrying and transport by rail of huge quantities of stone and the construction of a temporary workers' settlement. Known as 'Tin Town' on account of the corrugated metal used in much of its construction, this amounted to an industrial town in its own right, including a hospital, school, shops, police station and public bath-house in addition to the huts which provided temporary homes for a population of 900 working men and their families. As well as to Sheffield, the reservoirs supplied water to the industrial conurbations of Derby, Leicester and Nottingham.

Where the construction of large reservoirs was not a viable option, water was often stored under pressure in water towers. These can still be seen in many parts of Britain, and those constructed during the 19th century were often highly decorated. A good example is the castellated Gothic fantasy constructed at Shooter's Hill, one of a number of towers built to supply suburban London, which like many throughout the country became a local landmark. The Victorian period also saw the construction of water pumping stations by many municipal authorities. The pumps themselves were originally driven by steam engines, and those which survived into the 20th century were sometimes converted to power by electric generator. A superb surviving example of a steam-powered water pumping station is at Ryhope, near Sunderland in Tyne and Wear, where the main building, designed by Thomas Hawksley in 1868, took the form of a French baroque chapel.

*Water Tower
Shooter's Hill*

Sewerage became an urgent matter of concern in industrial towns and cities from the time that John Snow established the link between cholera and contaminated water supplies in the 1850s. In London Sir Joseph Bazalgette was responsible for the design of the Northern and Southern Outfall Sewers, whose construction between 1858 and 1865 is one of the supreme – if largely unseen and unsung – engineering achievements of the industrial age. By the start of the 20th century most major cities in Britain had sewerage systems, initially discharging straight into watercourses or the sea, but later to sewage treatment works.

EDUCATION AND IMPROVEMENT

The ownership of industrial facilities such as factories and mills brought with it the power to affect the lives of those who worked in them. All too often, inevitably, such influence was exercised in a negative manner. Happily, however, there was a sizeable body of enlightened industrialists who saw it as part of their work to seek improvement in the lot of their employees. One of the most famous examples was the social reformer Robert Owen. From the moment he entered into partnership with David Dale, the owner of New Lanark Mills, he wanted to improve the prospects for the 500 or so children who lived and worked on the site. As well as making arrangements for the older children, in

1816 he opened a school for infants, one of the first of its kind in Britain.

There had already been various independent efforts to look to the needs of the children of the industrial poor, many of whom were of course workers themselves. One of the earliest of these was the Sunday school movement. In 1785 a society was formed for the 'Establishment and Support of Sunday Schools throughout the Kingdom of Great Britain', and in 1803 the Sunday School Union was founded with the particular aim of improving provision made to the young inhabitants of London's slums. By the 1830s about a quarter of the country's children were enrolled in an institution of this type – some, like the Sunday school at Macclesfield, were in buildings whose regulated design was virtually indistinguishable from the mills in which they would live out their working lives. In the larger towns and cities there was additional support from the Ragged Schools, charitable bodies that provided for the industrial poor. Particularly influential were the Methodists, Quakers and other Nonconformist sects, and the crowded industrial landscape of many towns and cities is punctuated by their chapels. In 1797 the Methodist New Connexion was formed from congregations that wished to have greater control over their own affairs. Their appeal was principally to the industrial poor and their associations with political radicalism led to their being labelled 'Tom Paine Methodists' by many within the establishment.

As the industrial system tightened its grip on people's lives, it was vital for the established (Anglican) church to ensure that it did not lose out among the rapidly expanding factory towns. In 1818 the Church Building Act provided funds for the provision of new Anglican churches, particularly in the industrial towns. They were built especially in areas that had built up quickly owing to immigration of industrial workers. A good example is St Mary's Church, Bramall Lane, Sheffield, built between 1826 and 1829 on the edge of the rapidly developing industrial quarter known as 'Little Sheffield'. This fine building, designed in a perpendicular Gothic collegiate style, in fact attracted a congregation that was drawn more from the class of factory owners rather than workers.

Of more practical interest to the majority of working men were the Mechanics' Institutes. These first became a feature of the industrial scene in Scotland towards the end of the 18th century, after two University of Glasgow professors

St Mary's Bramall Lane

started to offer free lectures to workers in the city. One of these, George Birkbeck, eventually moved to London, where he founded the London Mechanics' Institute, which later became a constituent part of the University of London. In a similar development, in 1842 the Sheffield People's College was founded, open to both men and women for a fee of 1s 9d a week. Classes were held at 6.30am and 7.30pm in order to fit around the normal working day. Its success inspired the foundation of the Working Men's College in Queen Square, London, in 1854 and more than a dozen similar colleges were founded between 1855 and 1868 in England and two in Scotland.

In parallel with Birkbeck's foundation in London, Sheffield was also one of the earliest places where a technical school developed into a university. Sheffield Technical School developed out of local concern for better technical training of Sheffield's manufacturers and their employees, particularly those in the key steel industry. In 1879, local steel magnate Mark Firth had established Firth College as a centre for teaching arts and science subjects within the Cambridge University Extension Movement. Within Firth College itself a movement started to collect funds to create a technical department, established in 1884 as the Sheffield Technical School. In 1905 Firth College, Sheffield Technical School and the Sheffield School of Medicine amalgamated under royal charter as the University of Sheffield. Up until the First World War many of the courses were at non-degree level and included mining, razor grinding and railway economics.

A significant development in the newly opened coalfields of the later 19th century were the Miners' Institutes, which played a particularly important role within communities in South Wales and Scotland. Originally financed mainly by miners themselves, they catered for the need for self-improvement and general welfare among rapidly expanding populations. They generally contained reading and games rooms and, in time, rooms for showing films. From 1920 onwards they were supported by government grants. A fine example can be seen at Lochgelly, in Fife, which although built as late as 1923 was designed in an imitation Renaissance style intended to reflect its noble ambitions.

RECREATION

One of the consequences of the control that factory owners enjoyed over their workforce was that they started to demand an increasing say in what little free time the workers had. In the days before government legislation brought some limitations to the amount of time that could be demanded for work it was easier for employers to restrict the range of activities open to their workers. Essentially this would involve rudimentary education and religious worship, which suited the perceived need to maintain a disciplined workforce.

Although most industrialists recognised the need for recreation and refreshment, the 'gin craze' that gripped the 'lower classes' in the immediately pre-industrial era alerted many to the potential for social disorder. Whilst the influential temperance movement that developed at the time attempted to move against the use of alcohol altogether, the general view was that moderate consumption of more traditional brews was relatively harmless and provided strength to the arm of the working man. However, this was not a view always shared by their families, when wages were squandered in the beer house.

With extended free time came greater opportunities for recreation. Until the second half of the 19th century, however, this was restricted mainly to evenings, and the forms of diversion that became popular were those that evolved from the public houses that were the chief resort of the working man. Only when an increasing number of factory workers were given time off on Saturday afternoons could recreation take the form of organised sport, first in terms of participation and then, more significantly in the long term, as public spectacle. Throughout much of Britain this meant football, the remarkable popularisation of which owed much to the development of the railways and other forms of transport that allowed spectators to attend matches after work on Saturday mornings. And it was improvement in transport, too, that transformed the typical industrial worker's holiday from one spent at home in the 'pub' to a week's complete change of scene by the sea.

Beer Houses and Pubs

One of the most significant pieces of legislation in influencing the shape of working-class recreation for years to come was the Beer House Act of 1830 that allowed householders in England and Wales (as assessed for the poor rate) to retail beer and cider from their own houses on payment of an annual licence fee. The purpose of the legislation was to popularise beer among the working classes as an alternative to spirits such as gin. However, it was doubtful whether the authorities fully anticipated the rush to take up licences as soon as the legislation came into force on 24 October of that year. In Liverpool alone 50 new beer houses opened every day for much of the rest of the year. In England and Wales as a whole, within six months more than 24,000 new beer houses opened. In parts of some industrial cities, such as Sheffield, every sixth house in a street was licensed to sell beer.

Inevitably, concerns grew as to the effect on the health of working men, their home life and productivity. Such concerns were highlighted, for example, within the Sheffield cutlery industry where large numbers of men would take all of Monday off and spend the day and a large proportion of the family's income in beer houses and pubs. As a result, government at both local and national level became increasingly involved in the regulation of opening hours of licensed premises. In 1838 public houses in London were required to close between midnight on Saturday and noon on Sunday, and in 1848 this restriction was extended to the rest of the country. More legislation was introduced in 1855 and 1869 which, as further amended to ensure productivity among munitions workers during the First World War, stayed in force until the end of the 20th century.

Nevertheless, the connection between working-class communities and the consumption of beer had been established and remained a close one throughout the industrial era. Most intimately it is revealed in the early film footage shot at the gates of Lancashire factories in which workers are seen to emerge and take a drink from a portable beer stand set up to provide for their needs. More tangibly it is revealed in the numerous public houses that, despite recent large-scale closures in some parts, are still a prominent feature of the terraced streets of industrial towns and cities throughout Britain.

Music Hall
It was from the public houses that one of the most popular forms

of entertainment for the growing urban industrial populations developed. In London in the 1830s a new style of 'saloon bar' developed that became the venue for popular entertainments of a type which had formerly been on offer at traditional fairs and venues such as the Vauxhall Pleasure Gardens. The saloons either charged an admission fee or a higher drinks price at the bar in return for public singing, dancing, light drama and comedy acts. By the 1850s a number of so-called 'music halls' had developed, many of which had now become independent of their public house origins.

This form of entertainment was especially popular in London's East End, where a number of free-standing music halls were built for the staging of popular variety acts. By 1865 there were 32 music halls in London, seating between 500 and 5,000 people, plus a large number of smaller venues. The phenomenon peaked in 1878 when there were 78 large music halls in the capital and a number in other British towns. Attendances then declined, largely as a result of stricter licensing restrictions.

Nevertheless, music hall continued to be popular beyond the end of the First World War, while suffering increasing competition from the more widespread availability of pianos in even the poorest family homes, and the advent of radio, the gramophone and – the final coup de grâce – cinema (see p. 159). An outstanding surviving purpose-built music hall is the Hackney Empire dating from 1901.

Football

The most popular and enduring form of entertainment among the growing industrial populations was Association Football which, during the 19th century, migrated from the public schools to become the first modern mass spectator entertainment to rival the games of the ancient world. One of the earliest clubs to be formed was the Sheffield Football Club (1857) and this was followed by a number of others, particularly in the industrial Midlands and North of England where the game became increasingly popular among working men.

Problems arising from the growing professionalism of the sport led to the formation of the Football Association in 1865, and the need for organised fixtures resulted in the establishment of a Football League in 1888. Its original 12 members are a good reflection of the industrial geography of England at the time, with six clubs being based in Lancashire and six in the Midlands. With the admission of new members the league expanded rapidly, but it was not until the early 20th century that southern-based clubs made any impact, a result in part of the greater competition available from other forms of popular entertainment such as music hall.

For much of the 19th century, however, attendance at league matches, which cost 6d, was relatively expensive compared with a visit to the music hall, which would cost half that. As such, it was a little while after the formation of the Football League that the sport firmly established itself as a game for the industrial working classes. In fact, it has been argued that the League specifically maintained the 6d admission price in an attempt to keep out 'rowdier' representatives of the industrial population. In addition, many working men still faced the barrier of having to work on a Saturday. Even where some factories and trades were prepared to grant a half-day holiday, this did not allow much time for attendance at matches, even those of local teams.

It was the railways that eventually provided cheap and fast travel for football supporters, and by the early 20th century football and the railways had formed a lasting, if occasionally uneasy, relationship. When Chelsea Football Club was formed in 1905 the owners decided on a ground at Stamford Bridge on account of its proximity to Waltham Green station (now Fulham Broadway). Similarly, Manchester United moved to Old Trafford in 1909 to take advantage of the railway network established for the nearby cricket ground. In 1923 the final of the FA Cup competition was moved to the Empire Stadium at Wembley, which had also been sited mainly because of the excellent railway links. Over 270,000 people travelled in 145 special train services to the inaugural final.

By the end of the First World War football grounds had become a prominent feature of many industrial towns and cities, often looming up dramatically from among the terraced houses. Most of those used by professional clubs established before 1914 remained in use for much of the 20th century. The larger grounds were gradually improved. The large areas set aside for home supporters, often built on hills of ashes in the early part of the century, became concrete terraces or stands with seats protected by massive steel canopies. Many retained the name 'kop' (from the Afrikaans for 'hill'), a popular appellation deriving from the Boer War battle of Spion Kop, which had gripped the popular imagination at a time when football was reaching its heights of popularity. By then it had become a genuinely working-class form of mass entertainment, one that today remains an enduring legacy of a culture that developed in the burgeoning industrial towns and cities of Britain.

Cinema

The most prominent additions to the urban and suburban land-scapes of the first half of the 20th century were the cinemas. By 1914 there were about 3,000 picture houses, as they were then called, in Britain. Many had been established in buildings in previous use, such as corn exchanges and warehouses. Construction of purpose-built cinemas gathered pace in the 1930s. During the depression of that era it was noted that, like fish and chips, the cinema had become an important source of sustenance for the unemployed in industrial towns. George

Orwell noted famously, for example, that 'in Wigan the favourite refuge is the *pictures*, which are fantastically cheap there. You can always get a seat for fourpence at the matinees and at some houses you can even have a seat for tuppence. Even people on the verge of starvation will readily pay tuppence to get out of the ghastly cold winter afternoon.'

By 1938 there were nearly 5,000 cinemas in Britain, regularly frequented by almost half the population. Three companies dominated the medium – Associated British Cinemas (ABC), which in 1937 had 431 cinemas, Beaumont British which had 345, and Oscar Deutsch's Odeon which had 200. The auditoriums often had galleries like a traditional theatre and were typically steel-framed and clad with brick. The main entrances were commonly given eye-catching frontages in the contemporary art deco style. Like seaside holidays and attendance at football matches, cinema-going reached a peak in the years immediately after the Second World War. Following a decline in popularity during the 1960s and 1970s many cinema buildings of the earlier period were given over to bingo, a form of entertainment that had become popular particularly among working-class women.

Seaside Holidays – The Great Escape
One of the most socially significant changes to the lives of industrial workers was the gradual introduction of paid holiday, which occurred in the first half of the 20th century. In 1938, with the introduction of the Holidays with Pay Act, the principle was extended to most employees, though its implementation was delayed by the outbreak of the Second World War. Together with the extension of the railway network, this single piece of legislation transformed the nature of recreation for industrial workers in Britain. In the two decades following the end of the war this transformation was manifest in record numbers of

people taking seaside holidays. In July 1945, when a great proportion of the working population of the North of England was on holiday, 102,889 people are said to have arrived at the Lancashire resort of Blackpool alone – the largest number of arrivals that has ever occurred on a single day.

Day trips to the seaside from industrial towns and cities had already become popular by the second half of the 19th century, and much of the infrastructure of accommodation and entertainment that was to last through most of the 20th century was already in existence by 1900. Perhaps the most famous symbol of the seaside holiday, the Blackpool Tower, had been completed in 1894 during a decade when the average summer holiday population at the resort rose from 22,000 to 47,000. Constructed using 2,500 tonnes of wrought iron and 93 tonnes of cast steel, this iconic structure was itself a monument to the heavy industry in which many of the town's visitors worked. The Midland Hotel, built by the London Midland & Southern Railway at Morecambe in 1933, is thought to be the last hotel constructed by a railway company at a British seaside resort.

The peak in popularity of the British seaside holiday in the 1950s was greatly facilitated by improvements in rail transport. A number of seaside railway stations, such as Llandudno and Paignton, were enlarged and improved during the inter-war period. If the day trip had been the creation of the railways, its popularity was boosted after 1918 by the introduction of the motor coach. Days out by motor car, meanwhile, were available only to a minority before 1939, but became a mass experience in the immediate post-war period.

LIFE AND DEATH IN THE INDUSTRIAL TOWN

The continuing rapid progress of industrialisation throughout the 19th century had profound effects on the lives of the majority of the British population. Industrialisation brought with it large-scale urbanisation, which in turn created conditions of poverty and overcrowding that were ripe for the spread of disease. To give some idea of the scale of the changes, the population of Liverpool increased from 82,000 in 1807 to 202,000 in 1831, and this was before the large-scale immigration from Ireland following the potato famine of 1845.

Enormous pressures were put upon urban administrations, and these were only exacerbated by periodic outbreaks of epidemic disease, which disproportionately affected the industrial poor and their children. Cholera, a water-borne disease endemic in India, broke out in a number of British cities in 1831–2 and again in 1848. The first outbreak alone caused the deaths of around 53,000 people in England and Wales, the great majority drawn from the urban poor such as those commemorated in the prominent Cholera Memorial that keeps a melancholy vigil over the city of Sheffield.

Social reform, though slow, did come, and as we have seen a combination of private initiative and civic planning gradually provided clean water, sewerage and other facilities to the industrial towns and cities of Britain. At the national level, the Public Health Act of 1875 was just one of a number of measures introduced to improve the previously unsanitary conditions which blighted much of industrial urban living. In 1936 the novelist and broadcaster J.B. Priestley, commenting on the pall of smoke that seemed to hang perpetually over the colliery village of Shotton, County Durham, remarked: 'I hope it will always be there, not as a smoking tip, but as a monument to remind happier and healthier men of England's old industrial greatness.'

A notable development of the second half of the 19th century was the creation of infirmaries from the sick wards of workhouses. London had Poor Law Infirmaries from 1867, and other towns soon followed. They were a valuable addition to the charity and civic hospitals of the larger towns. An example of the situation that prevailed by the end of the 19th century was that in 1900 Sheffield had two hospitals that had grown from workhouse provision, an infirmary built by public subscription, a women's hospital provided by a private benefactor, a civic hospital and a mental asylum.

One of the most serious effects of the increase in urban populations that came with industrialisation was that provision for the disposal of the dead was soon found to be completely inadequate. Before the introduction of the Burial Acts of 1852 and 1853 most people were buried in church graveyards. By the middle of the 19th century, especially in those parishes whose populations had grown dramatically, overcrowding in churchyards had become almost as serious a risk to public health as that in housing. The Acts enabled local authorities to administer their own cemeteries, some of which they took over from private ownership. In Liverpool these included the Necropolis of 1825 and St James's Cemetery of 1829, the latter a landscaped disused quarry with processional ramps for funeral carriages and catacombs cut into the rock face.

One of the first public urban cemeteries in London was Kensal Green of 1827, a site covering 79 acres (32ha) with separate chapels for Anglicans and Dissenters. Other landscaped cemeteries followed, including Highgate (1839), Nunhead (1840), Abney Park and Stoke Newington (both 1840) and Tower Hamlets (1841). By the middle of the 19th century these cemeteries were run as commercial ventures, but after the passing of the Burial Acts enforcing the closure of urban churchyards municipal cemeteries became the rule.

Sheffield was typical of industrial towns, trebling in population from 45,758 in 1801 to 135,310 by 1851. Following a public outcry concerning the consequences of the town's overcrowded burial grounds Sheffield General Cemetery opened in 1836 and, in landscape terms, was seen as one of the most beautiful in the country. To one side there is a large area where there were deep plots for multiple pauper burials, the largest of which eventually contained 96 individuals, and in 1864 more than 60 victims of the disastrous Sheffield Flood (see p. 150) were buried in the grounds. In pride of place a small distance from these often unmarked graves are those of the town's leading industrialists, men such as the engineer John Parker (d.1845) and Mark Firth (d.1876), who established the largest steel company in Sheffield and on the strength of its success founded the technical college and later university. Urban cemeteries such as this are a key element of industrial landscapes and a forceful reminder of the type of society that was brought into being by industrialisation. Even in death, a clear hierarchy can be seen between the factory owners and their workers, twin pillars of the polarised society we call Industrial Britain.

WHAT NOW FOR INDUSTRIAL BRITAIN?

As we have seen, Britain has some of the most extensive remains of industrialisation in the world. These range from individual machines and buildings, through more complex sites to entire landscapes. Taken together, they represent an invaluable resource for understanding our recent past and the foundations of our present. Yet, as Britain becomes an increasingly post-industrial society, they also pose considerable problems. What should we preserve? What can be destroyed or allowed to decay? What is the best method of preservation? And, above all, how do we ensure that what remains has meaning for the generations to come?

TOWARDS AN APPRECIATION OF INDUSTRIAL HERITAGE

The first signs of a negative view being taken towards the country's industrial past are probably visible in the slum clearances that were initiated during the economic depression of the 1930s. For very good reasons the idea was formed in many people's minds that the inevitable result of industrialisation was dirt and disease. On top of this association, the genuine hardship that came with mass unemployment disinclined the majority to think sentimentally about industry and its machines, processes and buildings.

Yet the first murmurs of appreciation for the monuments of the Industrial Revolution could already be heard. By this time even some of the major canals and waterways had become uneconomical and were starting to silt up. A significant body of public opinion was alerted to the potential loss of a major component of national history, and in the years immediately following the end of the Second World War a remarkably successful campaign was launched to rescue Britain's canals for future generations.

A turning point in attitudes was reached with the demolition of the classical portico at Euston Station, London, in 1962. This had been one of the most powerful symbols of Stephenson's Birmingham to London railway of the 1830s, itself one of the great engineering achievements of the industrial age. It was, of course, just one of many demolitions that occurred between the 1950s and 1970s, carried out

Ironbridge Gorge

according to a policy of modernisation that, to many urban planners at least, seemed to demand starting with a clean sheet.

But just as this movement was in full swing in the 1960s, new methods of presenting historic buildings and landscapes to the public emerged, significantly influenced by the heritage movement that was developing in North America. These methods included visitor interpretation centres, heritage trails and brochure-style guides that were particularly well suited to industrial sites and monuments. Among the most successful applications of these ideas in Britain was the Ironbridge Gorge Museum that was established in the early 1970s in Shropshire in one of the heartlands of the Industrial Revolution. At around the same time another significant impetus to the emerging 'industrial archaeology' movement came from the commencement of restoration work at Richard Arkwright's famous factory at Cromford in Derbyshire by the newly formed Arkwright Society.

However, the acceptance of industrial archaeology as a serious and worthwhile discipline was neither universal nor immediate. In the words of one of its founding practitioners, Barrie Trinder, 'the industrial revolution was perceived rather like an ancestor who was both a philanthropist and a psychopath … the development of industrial archaeology in the twentieth century was not simply the growth of yet another academic sub-discipline but part of a process of coming to terms with a disturbing past'. It is ironic that until recently there was a much higher level of appreciation of the significance of Britain's industrial heritage from the other side of the globe than there was at home. It was the Japanese who led the way and flocked to sites like Ironbridge Gorge long before they became a tourist attraction to the British people themselves.

Change, when it came, was largely the result of the growing appreciation that Britain's situation was unique. Whether or not the notion that the industrial world was a British creation was accepted, there was little doubt that no other country was so rich in monuments of the industrial age and evidence of its impact on the landscape. Once it had been successfully argued that preservation of this heritage could be a positive element in regeneration projects, and the promotion of tourism, the way was clear for a significant change in public policy. The resulting creation of English Heritage and parallel bodies in the other parts of Britain in the 1980s created a level of statutory protection for the remains of the industrial past that, whilst not without its flaws, was unequalled in much of the rest of the industrialised world.

The more recent challenge has been to integrate the very recent industrial past into the general consciousness as something to take interest in and, where appropriate, to preserve. Such was the landscape dereliction caused by much of heavy industry that we have been left with a feeling – quite hard to shake off – that the 20th century was one big blot on the landscape that we need to tidy up after. A generation of industrial archaeologists who could find romance in a Newcomen engine and robust Britishness in the mills of New Lanark turned up their noses at the industrial estate and the oil refinery. Yet it is important that we come to terms with the final flourishing of the industrial system just as previous generations learned to love the Victorian factories and railway stations and to curb their desire to pull them down and replace them with concrete.

The significance of the industrial period in terms of world history was eloquently spelled out by Sir Neil Cossons in a pioneering synthesis of industrial archaeology in 1975 when he anticipated '… the awakening of an active appreciation that the remains of industrialisation in Britain are the tangible marks of the beginnings of a new civilisation which a thousand years hence the archaeologist and historian will identify, categorise, and possibly revere in the same way as we do the ancient cultures of the Mediterranean. With the industrial revolution period, however, we have the opportunity to keep the surviving remains alive because we are close enough to identify with the people who were involved.'

This is the second great challenge of the 21st century. Not only do we find ourselves in a unique position to preserve important remains of the very recent past, we have a unique ability to destroy them. Armed with massive earth-moving machinery, we now have the power to obliterate the physical evidence of the past on a scale that is without precedent. And while this is a power that is somewhat less likely to be unleashed against a medieval chapel or a Georgian mill, it can all too quickly be brought to bear against a bypass factory or the pithead gear of a redundant coal-mine. With this destructive power at our disposal – by which a massive coal-mine can disappear underneath a customer call centre virtually overnight – we have a particular responsibility as custodians of the recent past.

THE RISE OF INDUSTRIAL TOURISM AND THE OPEN-AIR MUSEUM

From the mid 1960s, largely through the efforts of industrial archaeologists and conservationists, industrial heritage had worked its way on to the tourist map. At about the same time, a number of prominent open-air museums were founded, including Ironbridge, Beamish and the Black Country Museum. It was also a time when enthusiasm for industrial narrow-gauge railways, which had developed in the post-war years, moved towards a more general appreciation of the need to preserve standard-gauge railways, then all the more pressing in the light of the Beeching Report aimed at severely reducing the extent of Britain's rail network. Within the space of a few years, this saw a number of preservation schemes established such as the Severn

Valley Railway, the Bluebell Railway in Sussex and the Great Western society at Didcot, Oxfordshire.

The initiative that was shown by private individuals and groups was, in the course of the next 20 years, taken up by local authorities in the main industrial cities. By the early 1980s museums of industry had been opened, for example, at Manchester, Sheffield, Leeds and Bradford at a time when living industry was in the first throes of almost terminal decline. The first of these municipal museums, that which opened in Birmingham in 1950, closed in 1998, an early pointer to the fact that industrial museums were no more immune to the vagaries of 'the market' than was industry itself.

For a time it seemed as though open-air museums would provide the solution to the problem of how best to conserve historic machinery, structures and buildings of the industrial period. From the start, however, the movement had its critics, who argued that it was best for industrial remains to be conserved, and interpreted, in their original context rather than being moved to museums. Such arguments gained strength when a number of structures, particularly in the North East and Midlands of England, were demolished on the promise of reconstruction at open-air museums, ambitious intentions that were either severely delayed or not implemented at all.

One of the most famous of the open-air museums, Beamish in the North East, attracted almost as much criticism as support over the years since its opening. To industrial archaeologists it was seen as a mixed blessing, since the funds it received by way of support from local authorities were inevitably diverted from application to heritage projects more generally. Just as seriously, local authorities now found it easier to remove support for monuments that the museum had declined to take into its care. As a result, it has been argued, there have been considerable losses of significant industrial heritage in the North East of England alone.

The area in which open-air museums were perhaps rather more successful has been in broadening the understanding of historical machinery, either through relocation of original examples, or by replication. Examples include the Newcomen engine at the Black Country Museum and the preservation of early steam locomotives at both Beamish and Ironbridge. However, the most ambitious of these projects, the reconstruction of a wrought-iron works at the Ironbridge Gorge Museum, has had a chequered history, and it could fairly be said that the lofty ambitions harboured for industrial museums at the outset – as laboratories for experimentation and interpretation – have only rarely been fulfilled.

At the same time, 'living' museums such as Beamish and the Black Country Museum have been criticised in some quarters for over-sanitising the past, presenting upcoming generations with an insight into a fantasy 'heritage land' rather than any historical reality. In particular, it has been argued that children leaving such museums after a day of witnessing, and participating in, historical re-enactments do so with little understanding of the social upheaval that came with industrialisation. Indeed, such presentations of the past highlight a central confusion in the national consciousness. On the one hand Industrial Britain represents a Dickensian indifference and cruelty that we feel glad to have left behind; on the other, it seems to embody a golden age of national and civic pride, together with an underlying spirit of philanthropy and public utility that we not only admire but wish we could revive.

REGENERATION THROUGH HERITAGE

In the final two decades of the 20th century a policy emerged of 'regeneration through heritage'. This developed from the recognition that conservation of redundant urban industrial buildings could play a useful role in revitalising inner cities devastated by the withdrawal of industry itself. In this way, empty buildings, rather than being simply demolished, could be a key part of maintaining community cohesion in a post-industrial world.

In its first incarnation, this movement led to the conversion of former industrial buildings at a number of sites into visitor attractions and local amenities. Some of these projects were on a large scale, such as the restoration in the early 1980s of Albert Dock, in Liverpool, following a long period of debate about its future and, more immediately, fears of social unrest following rioting in the Toxteth area of the city. The adaptation included new premises for the Merseyside Maritime Museum and an offshoot of the Tate Gallery, offices and retail premises. However, it is a sign of the transition of Britain from an industrial to a post-industrial society that the site is perhaps now more famous as the backdrop to the long-running *Good Morning* and *Richard and Judy* TV shows than as a jewel of the country's industrial heritage.

From large-scale projects such as this a policy developed of using listed-building and conservation-area powers to protect the architectural and historic integrity of former industrial sites by retaining groups of buildings within a meaningful context. A landmark implementation of this approach was the partnership between Birmingham City Council and English Heritage which led to the revitalisation of the city's famous jewellery quarter from the late 1980s. One of the key features of such schemes was to maintain the spatial relationships between industrial and domestic buildings such as those between a redundant mill and the houses of former workers, or the warehouses and port facilities of historic waterfronts.

Policies such as these were given added impetus following a survey in the early 1990s which revealed that former industrial buildings were particularly vulnerable to neglect and deterioration. This led to the formation of the Building Preservation Trusts, which played an important part in conserving historic industrial areas, such as the railway workers' houses at Derby and the concentration of workshop buildings at Kelham Island in Sheffield. Meanwhile, the importance of early intervention in avoiding irreparable damage to former industrial structures was demonstrated, for example, in efforts to safeguard historic warehouse facilities at Ellesmere Port.

Increasingly, from the 1990s through to the first decade of the 21st century, heritage regeneration schemes were focused more specifically on inner-city housing. Most commonly, this took the form of conversion of former mill and factory premises into apartment complexes, many of which were carried out with varied levels of success on former industrial sites particularly in lowland Scotland and northern England. In most cases it was merely the shell of the building that was maintained, with most of the internal arrangements being removed. Only in a minority of cases was much recognition given to the building's original function, exceptions including the conversion of some former workshop premises in Sheffield to use for light industry and warehousing. While purists frequently argued that residential conversions should only be accepted as a last resort, harsh reality usually meant either conversion to apartments or demolition.

Radical schemes voiced recently in some quarters, of relocating a substantial part of the population from what is perceived as a 'failing' old industrial North to a 'prosperous' South East, is just one extreme indication that the days of 'regeneration through heritage' might be numbered. This was given further emphasis by the reversal of the building boom and housing market preceding the economic recession that affected all areas of Britain at the end of the first decade of the 21st century.

THE CONSEQUENCES OF DEINDUSTRIALISATION

The coal-mining closure programme initiated in the later 1980s and early 1990s marked the beginning of what might be called a final phase of 'deindustrialisation' in Britain. The rapid pace of this process has presented those concerned with industrial heritage with particular problems of recording and conservation. At the same time it was increasingly recognised that the survival of at least a representative sample of industrial structures and landscapes was important in reflecting the transition from industrial to post-industrial society.

Unfortunately, however, planning policy tended to lag behind appreciation of the importance of former industrial landscapes. As a result, the survival of sites and features has often been a reflection of local rather than national priorities. So, for example, while textile mills – in some areas at least – have fared reasonably well, there has been wholesale destruction of sites associated with the iron and steel, shipbuilding and coal-mining industries throughout Britain. This means that entire industrial landscapes have often disappeared very quickly, leaving very little, if any, evidence of their former existence. In the case of coal-mining in particular, this often happens in the interests of 'cleaning up' apparently unsightly derelict landscapes.

At the same time, by the very nature of industrial decline, there is usually a need for rapid development of alternative employment opportunities. So, for example, the area of the former Manvers Colliery, near Rotherham in South Yorkshire, was rapidly transformed from one of the most productive mine workings in the country to one of the greatest concentrations of call centres in the UK. While local and national politicians joined in celebrating the creation of new jobs, nothing more than an abstract sculpture now marks the site of the former pithead gear, below which was one of the greatest complexes of mine workings in western Europe.

This obliteration of former industrial landscapes is, of course, to some extent inevitable. No society can, or does, stand still. In many cases extensive former industrial areas have been given over to new uses, which, like the Rotherham call centres, reflect the culture of the time in which they arose. In the mid 1980s, for example, the redundant Round Oak steelworks that had been at the centre of a vast industrial complex in the vicinity of Brierley Hill in the Black Country was closed. Within a few years the huge area of wasteland formerly occupied by the site had been transformed into the Merry Hill shopping centre, one of the largest of its type in the country.

A similar transformation is evident at Meadowhall in Sheffield's East End, where a massive retail complex has taken over much of the site formerly occupied by the heart of the country's iron, steel and armaments industries. A few miles away, the massive Templeborough Steelworks now provides the setting for a 'science and discovery centre' as well as occasional pop and techno music events. In the former industrial heartland of the North East of England, possibly no site better highlights the transition from industrial to post-industrial world than that of the former Wearmouth Colliery in Sunderland. Following closure in 1993, the site was redeveloped as the Stadium of Light, which provided a new home for Sunderland Football Club and its loyal following of supporters. Many of these had moved reluctantly from the club's original ground at Roker Park which, like many in Britain, had been situated in the middle of the terraced streets of this quintessentially industrial town.

THE IMPORTANCE OF CONTEXT

A significant milestone in the way Britain's industrial heritage is perceived was reached at the turn of the millennium when the government compiled a list of sites that might be nominated for UNESCO World Heritage status, effectively putting them on an equal level of significance with such icons of human achievement as the Pyramids of Giza. Acknowledging that one of the first World Heritage sites to be so designated in Britain was Ironbridge Gorge, in 1986, the government now proposed a tentative list that recognised 'the inception and process of industrialisation which has changed and moulded the way in which all the peoples of the world now live'. As such, industrial sites put up for consideration included the remains of the Cornish mining industry, the waterfront at Liverpool, the central textile manufacturing area of Manchester and those of the Derwent valley in Derbyshire, Saltaire and New Lanark Mills, sections of the Great Western Railway, the industrial landscape of Blaenavon, and the Pontcysyllte Aqueduct. All except Manchester and the GWR were approved by 2009.

While this goes a long way towards recognising the vital significance of industrial sites in Britain as a component of world history, just as importantly it reflects the need to view our industrial heritage in landscape terms rather than simply as individual monuments. At the same time, however, there is a danger of interpreting the industrial past as a series of landmark events rather than as an accretion of layers that need to be peeled back to reveal their true meaning and significance. Much of the social history of the past 250 years is bound up with landscapes that were first developed industrially in the 18th century and underwent constant change up to the end of the 20th.

To take just one example, the so-called Black Country in the

West Midlands was at the heart of the industrial development of Britain. Over the course of almost three centuries it saw the rise and fall of coal-mining, iron-making and a whole host of associated industries continually built upon the ruins of those that preceded them. As a result, superficially at least, there is little that remains apart from the canals that would indicate that this was a landscape developed industrially before the 20th century. It is therefore important that Britain's industrial heritage is not seen simply as a succession of individual monuments, but as a complex tapestry of interwoven elements that, taken together, can evoke something of the human experience of a relatively recent past as well as the foundations of the world in which we now live and which our successors will inherit.

PLACES TO VISIT

Please note that certain sites, such as converted factory premises, might be in private ownership and not available for internal inspection. Detailed information for all sites is available on the

ABERDEENSHIRE, SCOTLAND
Garlogie Mill Power House

ANGLESEY, NORTH WALES
Britannia Bridge

ANGUS, SCOTLAND
Caledonian Railway,
　Brechin
Verdant Works, Dundee

ARGYLL AND BUTE, SCOTLAND
Bonawe Iron Furnace

AYRSHIRE, SCOTLAND
Ballochmyle Viaduct

BEDFORDSHIRE, ENGLAND
Leighton Buzzard Railway

BRISTOL, ENGLAND
SS *Great Britain*, Great
　Western Dock
Museum of Bristol
Temple Meads Railway
　Station

CARMARTHENSHIRE, WALES
Kidwelly Industrial
　Museum

CHESHIRE, ENGLAND
Anderton Boat Lift
Chester Railway Station
Macclesfield Silk Museum
National Waterways Museum,
　Ellesmere Port
Quarry Bank Mill, Styal

CLWYD, WALES
Bersham Ironworks and
    Heritage Centre, Wrexham
Conwy Railway Bridge
Llangollen Railway
Minera Lead Mines,
    Wrexham
Pontcysyllte Aqueduct

CORNWALL, ENGLAND
Bodmin & Wenford Railway
East Pool Mine, Redruth
Geevor Tin Mine Museum,
    Penzance
Levant Mine and Beam
    Engine, St Just
Poldark Mine, Helston
Royal Albert Bridge, Saltash

COUNTY DURHAM, ENGLAND
Beamish: The Living
    Museum of the North,
    Stanley
Darlington Railway Museum
Killhope: The North of
    England Lead Mining
    Museum, Bishop
    Auckland
National Railway Museum,
    Shildon
Tees Cottage Pumping
    Station, Darlington

CUMBRIA, ENGLAND
Carlisle Citadel Station
Nenthead Mines Heritage
    Centre, Alston

DERBYSHIRE, ENGLAND
Belper, Strutt's North Mill
Calver Mill and Sough
Caudwell's Mill, Rowsley
Cromford Mill
Derwent and Howden
    Reservoirs
Lombe's Silk Mill (Derby
    Industrial Museum)
Magpie Mine, Sheldon
Masson Mill, Matlock Bath
Midland Railway Centre,
    Ripley
Moira Furnace Museum,
    Swadlincote
Pleasley Pit Head
The Silk Mill: Derby's
    Museum of Industry and
    History

DEVON, ENGLAND
Coldharbour Mill,
    Cullompton
Dartmouth Newcomen
    Engine
Dartmouth Steam Railway
Exeter (Haven Road) Power
    Station
Finch Foundry, Okehampton

Manor Mill and Forge,
    Branscombe
Morwellham Quay (former
    copper mine), Tavistock

DORSET, ENGLAND
Mangerton Mill, Bridport
Swanage Railway

DYFED, WALES
Gwili Railway, Carmarthen
Kidwelly Industrial
    Museum
Llywernog Silver-Lead Mine,
    Ponterwyd, Aberystwyth

EAST SUSSEX, ENGLAND
Bluebell Railway, Sheffield
    Park

ESSEX, ENGLAND
Colne Valley Railway, Castle
    Hedingham
East Anglian Railway
    Museum, Wakes Colne
Mangapps Railway Museum,
    Burnham-on-Crouch

FIFE, SCOTLAND
Forth Rail Bridge
    (connecting Edinburgh
    with Fife)
Lochgelly Miners' Institute

GLAMORGAN, WALES
National Waterfront
    Museum, Swansea
Rhondda Heritage Park

GLOUCESTERSHIRE, ENGLAND
Dean Forest Railway, Lydney
Gloucester Waterways
    Museum

GREATER LONDON, ENGLAND
Abney Park Cemetery
Battersea Power Station
Bankside 'B' Power Station
    (Tate Modern)
Craven Cottage Football
    Stadium
Hackney Empire
Highgate Cemetery
Kensal Green Cemetery
Markfield Beam Engine and
    Museum
Nunhead Cemetery
Shooter's Hill Water Tower
St Pancras Railway Station

*GREATER MANCHESTER,
    ENGLAND*
Astley Green Colliery
    Museum, Tyldesley
The Bolton Steam Museum
Castlefield (warehouses,
    canal)
East Lancashire Railway, Bury

Ellenroad Steam Museum,
Rochdale
Great Northern Railway
(GNR) Warehouse,
Manchester
Museum of Science and
Industry, Manchester

GWENT, WALES
Big Pit: National Coal
Museum, Blaenavon
Blaenavon Ironworks
Newport Transporter Bridge
The Winding House
Museum, Caerphilly

GWYNEDD, WALES
Sygun Copper Mine,
Beddgelert

HAMPSHIRE, ENGLAND
The Mid Hants Railway,
Alresford
Whitchurch Silk Mill

HERTFORDSHIRE, ENGLAND
Letchworth Garden City
Welwyn Garden City

INVERNESS, SCOTLAND
Glenfinnan Viaduct
Strathspey Steam Railway,
Aviemore

ISLE OF WIGHT
Isle of Wight Steam Railway,
Havenstreet

LANCASHIRE, ENGLAND
Blackpool Tower
Helmshore Mills Textile
Museum
Midland Hotel, Morecambe
Queen Street Mill Textile
Museum, Burnley

LANARKSHIRE, SCOTLAND
New Lanark
Summerlee: Museum of
Scottish Industrial Life,
Coatbridge
The Museum of Lead Mining,
Wanlockhead

LEICESTERSHIRE, ENGLAND
Abbey Pumping Station,
Leicester
Foxton Locks, Market
Harborough
Snibston Interactive Museum,
Coalville

MERSEYSIDE, ENGLAND
Albert Dock, Liverpool
Merseyside Maritime
Museum
Port of Liverpool and
Birkenhead Docks

Port Sunlight Model Village
St James Cemetery,
    Liverpool

Kew Bridge Steam Museum

MIDLOTHIAN, SCOTLAND
Scottish Mining Museum,
    Newtongrange

NORFOLK, ENGLAND
Fakenham Museum of Gas
    and Local History
North Norfolk Railway,
    Sheringham

NORTHAMPTONSHIRE,
    ENGLAND
The Canal Museum, Stoke
    Bruerne

NORTHUMBERLAND, ENGLAND
Cragside

NORTH YORKSHIRE, ENGLAND
Embsay and Bolton Abbey
    Steam Railway, Skipton
National Railway Museum,
    York
New Earswick
North Yorkshire Moors
    Railway, Pickering

NOTTINGHAMSHIRE, ENGLAND
Great Central Railway,
    Ruddington
Papplewick Pumping
    Station
Ratcliffe-on-Soar Power
    Station

OXFORDSHIRE, ENGLAND
Chinnor and Princes
    Risborough Railway
Didcot Railway Centre

SHROPSHIRE, ENGLAND
Ironbridge 'B' Power
    Station
Ironbridge Gorge Museums
    inc. Coalbrookdale, Blists
    Hill
Severn Valley Railway,
    Bridgnorth

SOMERSET, ENGLAND
East Somerset Railway,
    Shepton Mallet

SOUTH LANARKSHIRE,
    SCOTLAND
Biggar Gasworks

SOUTH YORKSHIRE, ENGLAND
Abbeydale Picture House,
    Sheffield
Cholera Memorial, Sheffield

Elsecar Heritage Centre (inc. Newcomen engine), Barnsley

Sheffield General Cemetery

Sheffield Industrial Museums, inc. Abbeydale Industrial Hamlet, Kelham Island Museum, Shepherd Wheel Workshop

St Mary's Church, Bramall Lane, Sheffield

Magna Science Adventure Centre (former Templeborough Steel Works), Rotherham

University of Sheffield Faculty of Engineering Buildings, Mappin Street, Sheffield

STAFFORDSHIRE, ENGLAND
Cheddleton Flint Mill

Etruria Industrial Museum, Stoke-on-Trent

Foxfield Railway, Blythe Bridge

Fradley (Canal) Junction

Gladstone Pottery Museum, Longton

Harecastle Tunnel, Kidsgrove

Stoke-on-Trent Railway Station

SURREY, ENGLAND
Airport House, Croydon (former Croydon International Airport)

TEESSIDE, ENGLAND
Middlesbrough Transporter Bridge

TYNE AND WEAR, ENGLAND
Dunston Staithes

The Bowes Railway, Gateshead

Derwentcote Steel Furnace, Rowlands Gill

Queen Alexandra Bridge, Sunderland

Ryhope Pumping Station

Tanfield Railway, Gateshead

WARWICKSHIRE, ENGLAND
Hawkesbury Engine House

WEST LOTHIAN, SCOTLAND
Bo'ness and Kinneil Railway

WEST MIDLANDS, ENGLAND
Austin Village, Birmingham

Back-to-back houses, Hurst Street/Inge Street, Birmingham (National Trust)

Birmingham Jewellery Quarter

Birmingham Railway Museum
    Trust
Black Country Living
    Museum, Dudley
Bournville Model Village
Curzon Street Railway
    Station, Birmingham

WEST SUSSEX, ENGLAND
Fernhurst Forge and Hammer
    Pond

WEST YORKSHIRE, ENGLAND
Armley Mills: Leeds
    Industrial Museum
Baildon Moor Bell Pits,
    Bradford
Bradford Industrial Museum
    (Moorside Mills)
Huddersfield Railway Station
Keighley & Worth Valley
    Railway

Middleton Railway, Hunslet
National Coal Mining
    Museum for England,
    Wakefield
Standedge Tunnels, Marsden
Saltaire
Thwaite Mills Watermill,
    Stourton

WILTSHIRE, ENGLAND
Caen Hill Locks, Devizes
Crofton Beam Engines,
    Marlborough
STEAM: Museum of The
    Great Western Railway,
    Swindon
Swindon 'Railway Village'

WORCESTERSHIRE, ENGLAND
Stourport Canal basins
Tardebigge Locks

SELECT BIBLIOGRAPHY

Buchanan, R.A.	Industrial Archaeology in Britain (Viking, 1974)
Burton, A.	National Trust Guide to Our Industrial Past (Mitchell Beazley, 1983)
Clark, C.	English Heritage Book of Ironbridge Gorge (Batsford 1993)
Cossons, N.	The BP Book of Industrial Archaeology (3rd revised edn, David & Charles, 1993)
Cossons, N.	Perspectives on Industrial Archaeology (Science Museum, 2000)
Dibnah, F. & Hall, D.	A Guide to Britain's Industrial Heritage (BBC, 1999)
Raistrick, A.	Industrial Archaeology: A Historical Survey (Paladin, 1973)
Stratton, M. & Trinder, B.	English Heritage Book of Industrial England (Batsford, 1997)
Stratton, M. & Trinder, B.	Twentieth Century Industrial Archaeology (Taylor & Francis, 2000)
Trinder, B.	The Making of the Industrial Landscape (W & N new edn., 1997)

SELECT GLOSSARY OF ARCHITECTURAL AND STRUCTURAL TERMS

art deco	Decorative style of the 1920s and 1930s characterized by use of bold geometric designs and strong colours
baroque	Extravagantly ornate style which first appeared in the 17th and 18th centuries
campanile	**Italianate** bell tower, often free-standing
classical/ neoclassical	18th–20th century revival of ancient Greek and Roman style characterised by principles of harmony and restraint in ornamentation
Corinthian	The most ornate of the classical orders of architecture characterised by flared column tops (capitals) decorated with acanthus leaves
dentilled	Decoration composed of small rectangular blocks
Diocletian	Semicircular window divided into three compartments
Doric	The least ornamented of the classical orders of architecture, characterised by plain, robust columns

façade	The main front of a building giving on to the street or other public space
faience	Moulded glazed blocks used mainly in decorative cladding
Gothic	18th-19th century revival of medieval style characterised by pointed arches and windows
Ionic	Classical order of architecture characterised by columns with scroll designs on either side of the capital
Italianate	Style of **neoclassical** architecture characteristic of the Italian renaissance
Jacobean	19th–20th century revival of a style prevalent during the reign of James I (1603–25) characterised by a blend of **classical** and **Gothic** features
Palladian	**Neoclassical** style prevalent in the first half of the 18th century, in part a reaction against the elaborate detailing of the **baroque**
pediment	Triangular feature of a **classical** building, usually above a window or door
pilaster	Rectangular column, usually projecting from a wall
portico	Projecting porch of a **classical** building
Queen Anne	20th-century revival of an early 18th century style characterised by use of red brick and simple rectangular design elements
quoin	Decorative cornerstone
Renaissance	**Neoclassical** architecture in the **Italianate** style
string course	A raised horizontal row of bricks, usually for decorative purposes

terracotta	Unglazed earth-coloured fired clay used as an ornamental building material
trunnion	Pivot on which a large receptacle is mounted
Tudor	19th and 20th century revival of the English **Renaissance** style
Venetian	Three-arched window associated with the **Palladian** style

INDEX